Innovations in Circular Economy and Net Zero

Olaniyi Evans · Ogechi Adeola

Innovations in Circular Economy and Net Zero

Strategies for Sustainable Growth in Emerging Markets

palgrave
macmillan

Olaniyi Evans
School of Management and Social Sciences
Pan-Atlantic University
Lagos, Nigeria

Ogechi Adeola
University of Kigali
Kigali, Rwanda

ISBN 978-3-032-22093-6 ISBN 978-3-032-22094-3 (eBook)
https://doi.org/10.1007/978-3-032-22094-3

This Palgrave Macmillan imprint is published by the registered company Springer Nature Switzerland AG
The registered company address is: Gewerbestrasse 11, 6330 Cham, Switzerland

Foreword

Emerging markets occupy a critical position in the global sustainability landscape. They are home to the world's fastest-growing populations and economies, while simultaneously facing disproportionate exposure to climate risks, resource constraints, and intensifying development pressures. As international commitments to sustainability and decarbonisation gain momentum, the pathways pursued by emerging economies will be decisive in shaping global outcomes across climate action, inclusive growth, and long-term resilience.

In *Innovations in Circular Economy and Net Zero: Strategies for Sustainable Growth in Emerging Markets*, **Olaniyi Evans and Ogechi Adeola** make a timely and important contribution to this evolving global agenda. Rather than presenting sustainability as a uniform or technocratic solution, the volume advances a context-responsive understanding of circular economy and net-zero transitions; one that recognises institutional diversity, uneven capacities, and the complex political-economic realities that characterise emerging markets. In doing so, the book moves beyond aspirational commitments to examine how sustainability strategies can be realistically designed, governed, and implemented in development contexts characterised by both constraints and opportunities.

A defining strength of this volume lies in its integrative perspective. The chapters collectively highlight the interdependence among policy frameworks, institutional capacity, innovation systems, and market dynamics. By bridging conceptual insight with policy relevance, the book clarifies why many sustainability initiatives struggle to achieve scale or durability and highlights the conditions under which circular economy and net-zero strategies can become credible drivers of sustainable growth rather than peripheral add-ons to development planning.

The volume is particularly compelling in its sustained focus on implementation. Through its examination of corporate practices, green financing mechanisms, digital and technological enablers, and regulatory instruments, the book identifies practical levers available to governments, businesses, investors, and development partners. Its emphasis on coordination across levels of governance underscores a critical insight: successful sustainability transitions in emerging markets depend less on isolated interventions than on coherent, multi-actor, and institutionally grounded approaches.

This book will be of considerable value to a wide audience, including policymakers seeking workable, evidence-informed sustainability frameworks; academics advancing research at the intersection of development and environmental governance; and practitioners engaged in innovation, investment, and inclusive growth across emerging economies. By situating circular economy and net-zero strategies within the lived realities of the Global South, the volume offers not only analytical clarity but also strategic direction, pointing towards pathways that are environmentally responsible, economically viable, and socially inclusive.

Bringing together robust analysis and forward-looking policy thinking, *Innovations in Circular Economy and Net Zero* stands as a timely and authoritative resource for those committed to shaping sustainable development trajectories in emerging markets and advancing a more resilient and equitable global economic system.

Prof. Felix Maringe, Ph.D.
Visiting Professor of Higher Education
University of the Witwatersrand
Johannesburg, South Africa

Independent Consultant
University of South Africa (UNISA)
Pretoria, South Africa

Preface

Emerging markets are at the heart of the global sustainability challenge, facing the overlapping pressures of climate change, socio-economic inequality, and underinvestment. This book, *Innovations in Circular Economy and Net Zero: Strategies for Sustainable Growth in Emerging Markets*, introduces the critical role of the circular economy and net-zero transitions as integrated solutions to these challenges. We explore global disparities in emissions, policy responses, and economic resilience, while examining the structural diversity of emerging economies. Drawing on institutional, innovation diffusion, and resource-based theoretical frameworks, we offer a systemic lens for understanding governance gaps, financial constraints, and technology adoption. We argue for an inclusive, adaptive, and context-sensitive pathway to sustainable development in the Global South.

The primary objective of this book is to examine the sustainability challenges confronting emerging markets and to propose integrated solutions through the lenses of the circular economy and net-zero transitions. Specifically, the book seeks to:

1. Highlight the circular economy and net-zero strategies as critical responses to climate change, socio-economic inequality, and chronic underinvestment.
2. Examine global disparities and structural variations in emissions, policy responses, and economic resilience across emerging markets.

3. Provide a systemic perspective on governance gaps, financial constraints, and technology adoption challenges.
4. Analyse the roles of digital technologies, corporate strategies, and green financing in enabling circular and net-zero transitions.
5. Assess policy and regulatory frameworks that support the adoption of circular economy models and net-zero targets.
6. Propose a multi-level, actionable policy roadmap and institutional strengthening strategies for effective implementation.

These objectives collectively aim to provide a comprehensive and actionable framework for achieving sustainable growth in emerging markets through circular economy and net-zero strategies. The book is organised into **three interrelated parts**, comprising **seven chapters**, with the final chapter serving as the conclusion, consolidating key insights and offering policy recommendations.

Part I: Conceptual and Technological Foundations

This first part lays the theoretical and technological groundwork for understanding circular economy and net-zero transitions in emerging markets. It reframes sustainability as a context-driven transformation process rather than a constraint, highlighting the dynamic interplay between local realities and global imperatives. The chapters explore how digital innovation, artificial intelligence, and other disruptive technologies are driving systemic change, enabling economies to leapfrog traditional industrial models and transition towards inclusive, low-carbon growth.

- Chapter 1: Reframing Sustainability in Emerging Markets: From Constraints to Context-Driven Transformation
  This chapter introduces the critical role of the circular economy and net-zero transitions as integrated solutions to the challenges faced by emerging markets. It explores global disparities in emissions, policy responses, and economic resilience, while examining the structural diversity of emerging economies. Using a systemic lens, it analyses governance gaps, financial constraints, and technology adoption—advocating for an inclusive, adaptive, and context-sensitive pathway to sustainable development in the Global South.

- Chapter 2: Digital and Disruptive Technologies for Net-Zero and Circularity in Emerging Markets
  This chapter examines the role of digital technologies in accelerating transitions to the circular economy and enabling net-zero development in emerging markets. It evaluates adoption conditions for key digital tools, including AI, blockchain, IoT, quantum computing, and digital twins. Institutional voids and regional disparities are highlighted, with proposals for inclusive strategies like regulatory sandboxes, green procurement, and public-private partnerships.

Part II: Pathways to Implementation

This part focuses on the practical dimensions of achieving circularity and net-zero goals. It examines the evolving role of the private sector, innovative financing mechanisms, and investment strategies that support sustainable transitions. Case studies and frameworks illustrate how businesses, investors, and cities are incorporating circular principles into their core operations. The chapters also spotlight critical sectors such as food systems and urban development, where policy alignment, innovation, and stakeholder engagement converge to create tangible sustainability outcomes.

- Chapter 3: Corporate Pathways to Net-Zero and Circular Economy Transition
  This chapter explores how emerging market firms pursue net-zero and circular economy goals amid institutional fragility, financing limits, and capability gaps. Using the resource-based view, it analyses how technological, financial, and human resources affect the credibility of climate commitment and its execution. The enabling roles of blended finance, innovation ecosystems, and adaptive policy are also highlighted.
- Chapter 4: Green Financing and Investment for a Sustainable Future
  This chapter examines how emerging markets can mobilise capital for green and circular economy transitions. It explores the role of financial instruments and institutions, applying institutional theory to evaluate how regulative mandates, normative expectations, and mimetic adoption shape sustainable investment ecosystems. Key barriers are identified, and proposed reforms, such as the use of fintech, regional cooperation, and capacity-building, are outlined.

- Chapter 5: Circular Economy in Food Systems and Urban Development
  This chapter examines the institutional, technological, and governance challenges that impede circular economy adoption in food and urban systems across emerging economies. It analyses how regulatory fragmentation, cultural norms, and informality impede circular economy strategies. The chapter concludes with recommendations for harmonised regional frameworks and multi-scalar approaches to enable equitable and scalable circular economy transitions.

Part III: Policy, Governance, and Future Directions

The final part addresses the enabling environment for circular and net-zero transitions, focusing on governance, regulation, and policy design. It analyses how national and international frameworks can accelerate systemic change, promote accountability, and align sustainability goals with economic growth. The concluding chapter synthesises insights across the volume and offers forward-looking recommendations for governments, institutions, and practitioners committed to driving sustainable transformation in emerging markets.

- Chapter 6: Policy, Regulation, and Global Implications for Circularity and Net-Zero
  This chapter examines how policies and regulatory frameworks facilitate the adoption of the circular economy and net-zero transitions in emerging markets. It analyses persistent governance barriers and highlights the necessity of adaptive, multi-level, and inclusive governance models. The chapter offers critical insights for policymakers seeking to operationalise circular economy and net-zero strategies within complex institutional environments.
- Chapter 7: Rethinking Governance for Circular Economy and Net-Zero Transitions in Emerging Markets: Conclusion and Recommendations
  In this concluding chapter, the book's core findings are consolidated. It is demonstrated that the success of circular economy and net-zero transitions in emerging economies depends on regulatory capacity, governance coherence, and institutional legitimacy. A multi-level,

actionable policy roadmap and institutional strengthening strategies are presented, with emphasis on context-sensitive, inclusive, and capacity-focused governance reforms.

Overall, this book underscores that effective implementation of circular economy and net-zero transitions in emerging economies is contingent upon regulatory capacity, coherent governance, and institutional legitimacy. It offers practical guidance through a multi-level policy roadmap and institutional reform strategies, highlighting the importance of inclusive and adaptive approaches tailored to local contexts.

Taken together, the three parts of this book provide an integrated roadmap that bridges conceptual frameworks, technological innovation, corporate strategy, and governance reform. By combining theoretically informed insights with actionable recommendations, it demonstrates that sustainable growth in the Global South is attainable when innovation, policy coherence, and inclusivity align. This book will be of particular interest to policymakers, academics, business leaders, investors, NGOs, and technology innovators engaged in sustainability, the circular economy, and net-zero transitions in emerging markets.

Lagos, Nigeria — Olaniyi Evans
Kigali, Rwanda — Ogechi Adeola

Acknowledgements We extend our sincere gratitude to our colleagues and students at Pan-Atlantic University, Nigeria and the University of Kigali, Rwanda, for their insightful feedback and intellectual engagement throughout the development of this book. We are thankful to the Palgrave team for their editorial guidance and to the anonymous reviewers whose thoughtful comments helped strengthen the manuscript.

We extend our deepest appreciation to our families for their steadfast support, encouragement, and patience. We are also indebted to the global community of researchers and practitioners who continue to advance the frontiers of circular economy and net-zero transitions; your work inspires and informs this contribution.

Competing Interests The authors have no competing interests to declare that are relevant to the content of this manuscript.

Contents

About the Authors

Olaniyi Evans is a Senior Lecturer in Economics at Pan-Atlantic University, Lagos, and a leading Nigerian scholar on digital economies, green finance, and inclusive growth. He holds a PhD, an M.Sc. with Distinction, and a First-Class B.Sc. in Economics from the University of Lagos. Evans has published extensively in leading international journals and authored several influential books, including "Gender Equality, Climate Action, and Technological Innovation for Sustainable Development in Africa." He has received several academic distinctions, including the Emerald Literati Award and the University of Lagos Certificate of Excellence. In 2025, he was named on the Stanford University–Elsevier Top 2% Scientist List, which recognises the world's most impactful researchers based on citation metrics. As Managing Editor of *BizEcons Quarterly*, he mentors emerging scholars and advances policy-relevant economic research that informs sustainable development discourse across Africa and other emerging regions.

Ogechi Adeola is Professor of Marketing and Deputy Vice-Chancellor at the University of Kigali, Rwanda, and Adjunct Professor at Torrens University Australia. She is an internationally recognised scholar with over 150 academic publications, specialising in marketing, sustainability, digital transformation, circular economy, and inclusive development in Africa. She co-authored the book Gender Equality, Climate Action, and Technological Innovation for Sustainable Development in Africa (2021), a seminal volume that explores pathways toward a more equitable and sustainable future. Her research has garnered several awards, including Best Paper Awards at global conferences (2016–2019), and the Emerald Literati Award for Outstanding Paper in 2022. In 2025, she was ranked among the top 2% of scientists worldwide in the Stanford University–Elsevier list, reflecting her significant contributions to sustainability and development research in Africa. Beyond academia, she has consulted for institutions such as Afreximbank, the International Labour Organization, and the International Institute of Tropical Agriculture (Business Incubation Platform), with expertise spanning trade development, women's empowerment, and sustainable innovation.

List of Figures

List of Tables

PART I

Conceptual and Technological Foundations

CHAPTER 1

Reframing Sustainability in Emerging Markets: From Crisis to Context-Driven Transformation

Abstract Emerging markets are at the heart of the global sustainability challenge, facing the overlapping pressures of climate change, socio-economic inequality, as well as underinvestment. In this chapter, we introduce the critical role of the circular economy and net-zero transitions as integrated solutions to these challenges. We explore global disparities in emissions, policy responses, and economic resilience, while simultaneously examining the structural diversity of emerging economies. Drawing on institutional, diffusion of innovation, and resource-based theoretical frameworks, we offer a systemic lens for understanding governance gaps, financial constraints, and technology adoption. We argue for an inclusive, adaptive, and context-sensitive path to sustainable development in the Global South.

Keywords Sustainability · Emerging markets · Circular economy · Net-Zero transitions · Climate change · Policy gaps · Socio-economic development · Technology adoption

O. Evans and O. Adeola, *Innovations in Circular Economy and Net Zero*, https://doi.org/10.1007/978-3-032-22094-3_1

1.1 Global Sustainability Challenges and the Need for Transformative Solutions

The trio of climate instability, ecological degradation, and rising inequality represents an urgent global sustainability crisis. Each of these challenges compounds the others, undermining human security and ecological resilience across regions. Current processes, dominated by carbon-intensive growth and unequal access to resources, continue to exacerbate both planetary boundaries and socio-economic divides (Environmental Justice Foundation [EJF], 2022; Feffer, 2025). These systemic threats require systemic solutions. Specifically, integrated approaches, such as the circular economy and net-zero transitions, can transform production, distribution, and governance on a global scale.

1.1.1 *Climate Breakdown and Structural Inequality*

Climate change is no longer a distant threat; it is now defining global development. The earth's surface temperature has already risen by 1.1 °C above the pre-industrial average, with a trajectory towards 2.7 °C by the end of the century unless mitigation efforts accelerate (EJF, 2022). Climate-related disasters displaced over 30.7 million people in 2020 alone, and projections suggest that up to 132 million more may fall into extreme poverty by 2030 due to escalating climate shocks (EJF, 2022). These impacts fall hardest on those least responsible for emissions. The bottom half of the world's population contributed only 7% of the cumulative carbon emissions from 1990 to 2015, whereas the wealthiest 10% generated 52% (EJF, 2022).

The distribution of historical emissions also reveals a deep-rooted climate debt. Between 1751 and 2021, the United States accounted for approximately 25% of cumulative carbon emissions, with the European Union contributing 22% (Feffer, 2025). In stark contrast, all regions, such as sub-Saharan Africa, Southeast Asia, and Oceania, are marginal emitters despite bearing the brunt of climate-induced losses. As of 2023, experts estimated that only 250 gigatonnes of carbon remain in the global budget to limit warming to 1.5 °C, with China accounting for a significant share of global emissions by 2021 (Feffer, 2025).

Stark inequalities exist in both the impacts of climate change and responsibility for emissions across global income groups. Figure 1.1 reveals a paradoxical imbalance: while the bottom

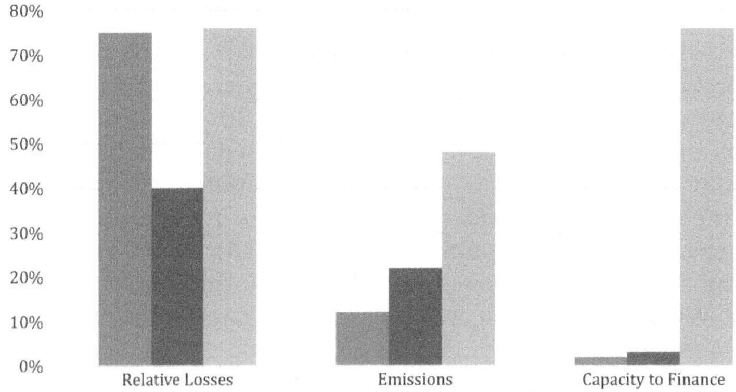

	Relative Losses	Emissions	Capacity to Finance
Bottom 50%	75%	12%	2%
Middle 40%	40%	22%	3%
Top 10%	76%	48%	76%

Fig. 1.1 Global climate inequality: relative losses, emissions, and capacity to finance (*Data source* World Inequality Lab [2023])

50% and top 10% bear similarly high relative income losses from climate change (75% and 76%, respectively), their contributions to emissions and capacity to mitigate climate impacts diverge dramatically. The top 10% emit 48% of greenhouse gases and hold 76% of global wealth, underscoring their disproportionate role in driving the crisis and their unmatched ability to fund solutions. Despite facing severe losses, the bottom 50% contribute just 12% of emissions and hold only 2% of wealth. This highlights systemic inequities in climate vulnerability and economic power.

1.1.2 Policy Gaps, Inequities, and Regressive Measures

While international climate frameworks acknowledge these disparities, global responses have not fulfilled expectations. High-income countries pledged to mobilise $100 billion annually for the mitigation and adaptation efforts of developing countries. However, as of 2025, only $28 billion per year has been realised (Feffer, 2025). The 2022 "loss and damage" fund for climate-vulnerable nations received pledges amounting to less than $1 billion, which is significantly below the $290–$580 billion required annually by 2030 (Feffer, 2025). Although countries increased their pledges to $300 billion annually by 2035 at the 2024 Baku conference, the majority of these funds are in the form of loans, thereby exacerbating sovereign debt (Feffer, 2025). Furthermore, mitigation mechanisms such as carbon taxes and emissions trading schemes often produce inequitable outcomes. For example, France's fuel tax reforms in 2018 incited widespread protests due to their perceived unfairness to low-income communities (Pande, 2023). As of 2022, emissions trading schemes encompassed only 17% of global greenhouse gas emissions. While they establish credible emissions targets, they frequently fail to equitably distribute costs and benefits (Pande, 2023). Fossil fuel subsidies, which surpassed $1 trillion globally in 2022, exacerbate this issue by disproportionately benefiting wealthier individuals who consume more energy (Pande, 2023).

1.1.3 The Role of Circular Economy in Achieving Systemic Transformation

To avoid reinforcing these inequities, policy instruments must incorporate distributional impact assessment. Transformative solutions must simultaneously mitigate the environmental impacts and address socioeconomic disparities. The circular economy offers a compelling paradigm shift by reducing dependence on virgin resources, minimising waste, and recirculating materials across economic systems. Empirical evidence from 29 European countries indicates that adopting a circular economy results in a significant reduction in CO_2 emissions and improves environmental quality (Hailemariam & Erdiaw-Kwasie, 2022). Moreover, the circular economy contributes to resilience through local value chains, decentralised resource flows, and regenerative production.

The current implementations of the circular economy often prioritise economic efficiency while marginalising environmental and social dimensions (Hassan & Faggian, 2023). A truly systemic circular economy must apply transdisciplinary frameworks and account for behavioural, financial, and institutional drivers (Khalifa et al., 2022). As Fragkos (2022) highlights, integrating a circular economy with energy efficiency reduces industrial emissions, lowers dependence on costly technologies such as carbon capture, and facilitates cost-effective decarbonisation.

Emerging economies can leverage circular economy strategies to promote inclusive growth when supported by equitable partnerships.

For example, Chile, a major lithium producer, has begun using its resource leverage to negotiate stronger control over value chains, rather than relying solely on extractive exports (Feffer, 2025). Similarly, South Africa's Just Energy Transition Partnership mobilises international finance while prioritising worker retraining and local industrial development. These cases show how a circular economy embedded in justice-based frameworks can provide countries with developmental alternatives.

1.1.4 Emerging Markets and the Geopolitics of Transition

Emerging markets face the triple constraints of chronic underinvestment, entrenched structural inequality, and heightened exposure to climate-related shocks. Yet, they also possess a unique opportunity to redefine the trajectory of global sustainability. Several countries have already demonstrated leadership in climate policy and energy transition. Uruguay, for instance, now sources over 95% of its electricity from renewable sources, establishing a model for low-carbon energy systems in the Global South (Feffer, 2025). Similarly, Indonesia's proposal to coordinate nickel exports and India's ambitions to become a global hub for green hydrogen signal a shift towards asserting agency in sustainable industrial policy. However, resource endowments alone cannot deliver transformative outcomes. Realising the full potential of these transitions will depend on meaningful commitments from the international community, particularly in ensuring equitable access to climate finance, technology transfer, and fair-trade frameworks. Without these structural enablers, global net-zero and circular economy narratives risk becoming aspirational rhetoric rather than actionable pathways.

The sustainability imperative is increasingly reshaping strategic priorities in emerging markets, particularly with respect to climate resilience and decarbonisation. Hundreds of large firms have pledged to achieve net-zero emissions, and around half of all publicly traded companies in these economies explicitly incorporate climate impacts into their financial disclosures (Tansan et al., 2023). Notable corporate examples include Alibaba and Tencent in China, both targeting net-zero by 2030; Natura in Brazil, carbon–neutral since 2007; Infosys in India, which reached carbon neutrality in 2020; and Sasol in South Africa, which plans to reduce CO_2 emissions by 30% by 2030 and achieve net-zero by 2050. At least 35 governments across emerging markets have also made national carbon neutrality commitments (Tansan et al., 2023). The urgency of

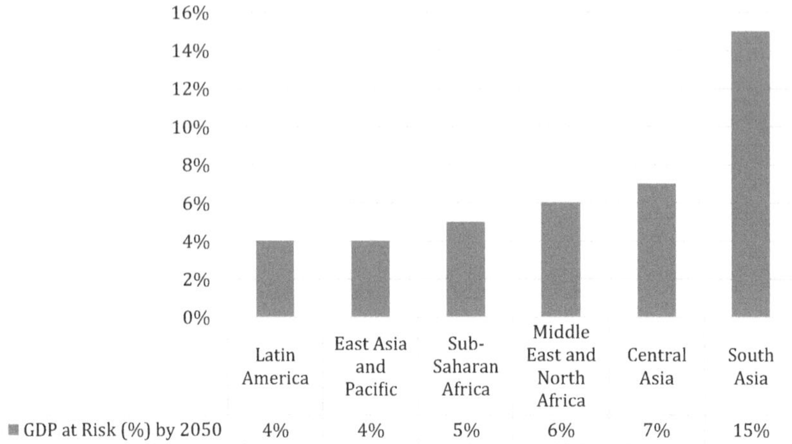

Fig. 1.2 GDP at risk (%) by 2050 (*Data source* Tansan et al. [2023]. The data highlights the regional disparities in climate vulnerability)

these pledges stems from the disproportionate climate vulnerability faced by these nations (see Fig. 1.2), which, despite lower per capita emissions, experience more severe impacts such as extreme weather events, biodiversity loss, and economic disruption. If left unaddressed, climate change could erode up to 15% of per capita GDP in South Asia by 2050 (Tansan et al., 2023). Emerging markets, which account for about 70% of the world's population and 50% of global GDP (World Bank, 2021), must adopt innovative, low-emission development models that decouple growth from environmental degradation. The global community must support this pivot to avert worsening climate inequities and to ensure a sustainable future.

1.2 The Emerging Markets Landscape: Complexity, Heterogeneity, and Global Interdependencies

Emerging markets comprise a diverse set of economies. They share some transitional traits but differ significantly in development and structure. Defined broadly by institutions such as the International Monetary

Fund (IMF) and MSCI, these markets encompass countries progressing towards industrialisation, greater integration with global trade and finance, and expanding middle-class populations, yet lack the institutional stability and income levels of advanced economies (Stripe, 2025). Sub-Saharan Africa, Southeast Asia, and Latin America are typically grouped as emerging markets, and substantial heterogeneity within and across these regions challenges any notion of economic uniformity.

Governance capacity and institutional quality constitute a critical source of differentiation. Countries such as Malaysia and Vietnam in Southeast Asia demonstrate relatively effective regulatory environments and coherent industrial policies. By contrast, many sub-Saharan African nations grapple with fragmented institutions and weak governance structures that impede the implementation of large-scale industrial or digital development strategies (World Bank, 2024). Latin America is a mixed institutional landscape; Brazil and Chile illustrate stronger democratic frameworks, whereas Argentina and Venezuela continue to face chronic governance instability (Andaman Partners, 2025). Government effectiveness encompasses the assessment of the quality of public services, the calibre of the civil service and its autonomy from political influences, the quality of policy development and execution, as well as the reliability of the government's commitment to these policies (World Bank, 2025). As shown in Fig. 1.3, India's government effectiveness improved significantly between 2015 and 2023 (from 0.08 to 0.48), while Vietnam also witnessed modest gains (from 0.06 to 0.13), indicating better governance over time. Brazil, Argentina, and South Africa experienced notable declines, with Brazil falling from −0.26 to −0.55 and Argentina from −0.05 to −0.38, reflecting worsening governance perceptions. These patterns reinforce the need for targeted governance reforms, institutional strengthening, alongside policy coherence as foundational pillars of development in emerging markets.

Industrial structures further emphasise this diversity (Fig. 1.4). Southeast Asian economies, such as Vietnam, have leveraged manufacturing- and export-oriented industrial policies to integrate into global value chains. In contrast, Sub-Saharan Africa is predominantly reliant on primary commodity exports, with limited value addition. Latin America (e.g., Brazil and Mexico) maintains a more diversified economy that blends agriculture, energy, and industrial production (Grynspan, 2025). Digital infrastructure development also mirrors this asymmetry. In Sub-Saharan Africa, internet access expanded rapidly between 2016 and 2021,

	Argentina	Brazil	Mexico	Nigeria	South Africa	Kenya	India	Pakistan	Viet Nam
2015	-0.05	-0.26	0.12	-1.00	0.09	-0.39	0.08	-0.71	0.06
2023	-0.38	-0.55	-0.20	-0.85	-0.26	-0.30	0.48	-0.58	0.13

Fig. 1.3 Government effectiveness (*Data source* World Bank [2025]. The estimate gives the country's score on the aggregate indicator, in units of a standard normal distribution, i.e., ranging from approximately −2.5 to 2.5)

with the region recording a 115% increase in internet users. Over 160 million new broadband connections were added between 2019 and 2022 (World Bank, 2024). However, connectivity remains a challenge, particularly in rural areas, exacerbated by affordability and a persistent digital gender divide. Uganda's broadband expansion and Malawi's provision of affordable internet to 4.3 million people illustrate targeted interventions, but such advances are uneven across the continent (World Bank, 2024). Conversely, Southeast Asia's relatively advanced digital infrastructure supports fintech, digital education and e-commerce, although digital exclusion persists among lower-income populations (Bislimi et al., 2024)

.

Emerging markets' integration into global trade networks also displays uneven patterns (see Fig. 1.5). According to recent trade data, Asia exported USD 7.14 trillion worth of goods in 2023, with 51% within the region, reflecting robust intra-regional trade ties. In contrast, Sub-Saharan Africa exported goods worth $356 billion in the same period, of which only 22.3% involved intra-African trade (Andaman Partners, 2025). This contrasts sharply with Europe, where over 70% of exports circulate within the region. Latin America reported a similar trade pattern. Of its USD

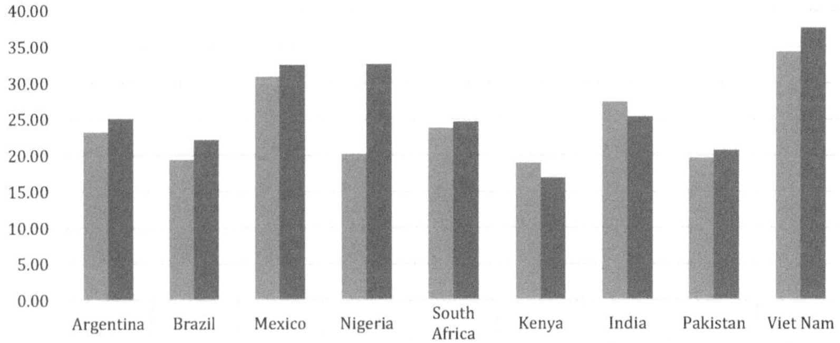

	Argentina	Brazil	Mexico	Nigeria	South Africa	Kenya	India	Pakistan	Viet Nam
2015	23.15	19.36	30.84	20.16	23.73	18.89	27.35	19.60	34.27
2023	25.06	22.14	32.48	32.58	24.62	16.86	25.30	20.66	37.58

Fig. 1.4 Industry (including construction), value added (% of GDP) (*Data Source* World Bank [2025])

764 billion in exports, only 20.5% was traded within the region, with Asia (37.1%) and North America (20%) as its principal external partners (Andaman Partners, 2025). These patterns expose Sub-Saharan Africa and Latin America to external economic shocks, currency volatility, alongside fluctuations in commodity demand.

Investment flows highlight additional dimensions of global interdependence. Investor confidence in the Asia-Pacific and Latin America surged in 2025, reflected by a 15% increase in the S&P Emerging BMI Index, driven by perceived opportunities in supply chains and regional diversification (Lazzaro, 2025). India's case exemplifies this trend with recorded foreign direct investment (FDI) inflows exceeding US$50 billion in FY 2024–2025, concentrated in manufacturing, infrastructure, and agriculture (Rao, 2025). Southeast Asia, particularly Vietnam and Indonesia, similarly attracted investment, as multinational corporations sought alternatives to China in response to tariff pressures and geopolitical risks. For example, Argentina and South Africa witnessed FDI increases between 2015 and 2023 (Fig. 1.6), with Argentina's FDI rising from 1.98% to 3.69%, suggesting improved investor confidence. India, Mexico, and Brazil experienced declines, with India's FDI dropping sharply from 2.09% to 0.77%, possibly due to global economic shifts or domestic policy changes. Sub-Saharan Africa remained comparatively marginalised

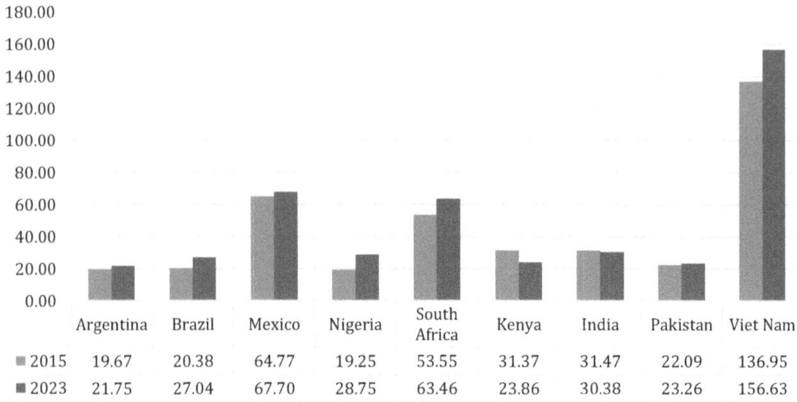

Fig. 1.5 Merchandise trade (% of GDP) (*Data Source* World Bank [2025])

in global capital flows, constrained by infrastructure deficits, weaker governance frameworks, and higher perceived investment risk (World Bank, 2024).

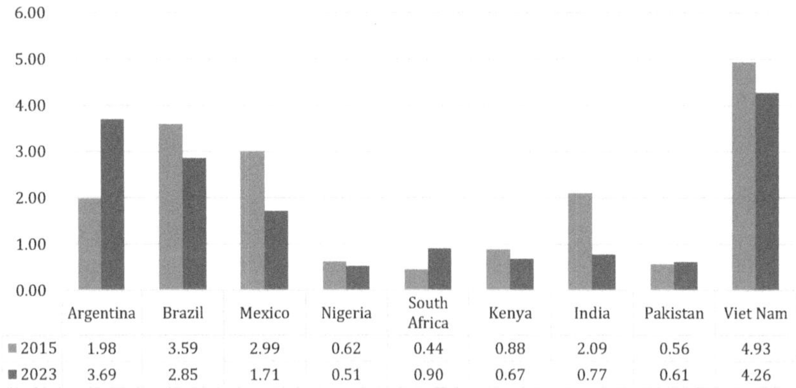

Fig. 1.6 Foreign direct investment, net inflows (% of GDP) (*Data Source* World Bank [2025])

Debt obligations intensify these vulnerabilities. Emerging markets collectively face $400 billion in external debt repayments in 2024, a burden that risks diverting fiscal resources from digital transformation, infrastructure investment, and climate adaptation (Mammadov, 2025). Much of this debt is denominated in foreign currencies, exposing countries to exchange-rate volatility and higher refinancing costs amid global interest-rate uncertainty. Sub-Saharan Africa, in particular, faces compounded debt and climate finance challenges that constrain its fiscal flexibility to invest in sustainable growth. Many countries in the region also rely heavily on concessional financing and face shrinking fiscal space due to rising debt-servicing costs (Karlin & Sierra-Escalante, 2021), which crowd out public investment and constrain policy responses to social and environmental priorities.

Climate commitment and global frameworks further complicate the developmental trajectories of emerging markets. Africa's adaptation financing needs for 2020–2030 are estimated to range from $259 billion to $407 billion, while mitigation financing requirements totalled approximately $715 billion (Integral Consult, 2021). However, limited access to international climate finance constrains progress. Consequently, carbon markets have emerged as alternative financing mechanisms. African countries (for example, Kenya and Ethiopia) have utilised reforestation and agroforestry projects to generate carbon credits, producing over 150,000 and 200,000 credits respectively (Hachileka, 2025). Ghana has advanced carbon market integration by completing trades under the Paris Agreement's Article 6.2, which signals the institutional capacity for market-based mitigation (Hachileka, 2025). Nevertheless, Africa's broader participation remains restricted: only nine countries have comprehensive legal frameworks for carbon trading, while most lack digital monitoring systems and transparent registries, undermining equitable benefit-sharing and limiting investor confidence (Hachileka, 2025).

Trade policies, such as the European Union's Carbon Border Adjustment Mechanism (CBAM), further highlight the structural asymmetries that confront emerging markets. While CBAM aims to reduce carbon leakage by imposing tariffs on carbon-intensive imports, it inadvertently penalises export-dependent economies (particularly in Southeast Asia, Latin America, and parts of Africa) that lack the capital and infrastructure required for low-emissions manufacturing (Law & Fong, 2025). For example, aluminium and steel producers (e.g., Indonesia, Mexico) face potential losses of export competitiveness unless they can transition to cleaner production methods. However, it is difficult to replicate the carbon pricing frameworks of advanced economies. Although China's national emissions trading scheme and South Korea's cap-and-trade system offer regulatory models (Legal Response International, 2022), these mechanisms depend on robust digital infrastructure, institutional enforcement, and policy coherence, features that are often underdeveloped in many lower-capacity emerging markets.

In numerous regions across Africa and Southeast Asia, inadequate governance and limited emissions data impede the establishment of transparent registries and reliable reporting mechanisms. The fragmented nature of industrial sectors complicates the development of emissions-tracking tools, which are crucial to the functioning of carbon markets (World Bank, 2023). As a result, these countries face vulnerabilities and a loss of competitiveness under the Carbon Border Adjustment Mechanism (CBAM), while lacking the necessary tools to engage in the global carbon trade. The compliance and administrative demands of CBAM disproportionately affect small and medium enterprises (SMEs), particularly those operating within semi-formal or informal sectors (World Bank, 2023). In the absence of targeted support, such as concessional finance, carbon accounting infrastructure, and training, many emerging markets risk exclusion from green trade frameworks and may become entrenched in carbon-intensive sectors.

1.3 Circular Economy and Net-Zero Transitions: Path to Sustainable Growth

Comparative data highlighted significant variations in urban performance across the six critical indicators of circularity (Fig. 1.7). The data reveal fragmented circular transitions, with a few cities achieving synergy between environmental stewardship, social innovation, and infrastructure readiness. Achieving net-zero emissions by 2050 requires more than an energy transition. A circular economy, defined as a restorative and regenerative economic system that eliminates waste, keeps products and materials in use, and regenerates natural systems, provides a major complementary path (Charnley, 2022). This approach extends beyond traditional climate strategies, which focus on renewable energy and energy efficiency. According to the Ellen MacArthur Foundation, clean energy transitions account for only 55% of global emissions, with the remaining 45% arising from the production of goods and materials that underpin modern economies (Charnley, 2022). Thus, circular economy principles aim to reduce emissions associated with material production, consumption, and disposal systems.

The circular economy model rests on three principles: elimination of waste and pollution, circulation of products and materials at their highest value, as well as regeneration of natural capital (Charnley, 2022). These principles support decarbonisation by reducing the demand for virgin materials and lowering emissions across entire value chains. Industrial applications demonstrate the importance of a circular economy for net-zero transitions. Heavy industries, like steel, cement, aluminium, and chemicals, make up 27% of global CO_2 emissions, releasing about 7.1 gigatonnes each year (World Economic Forum, 2019). Demand for these materials is rising, especially in emerging economies that are developing infrastructure and urbanising. Current strategies that focus solely on clean energy and production efficiency cannot mitigate this growth in emissions.

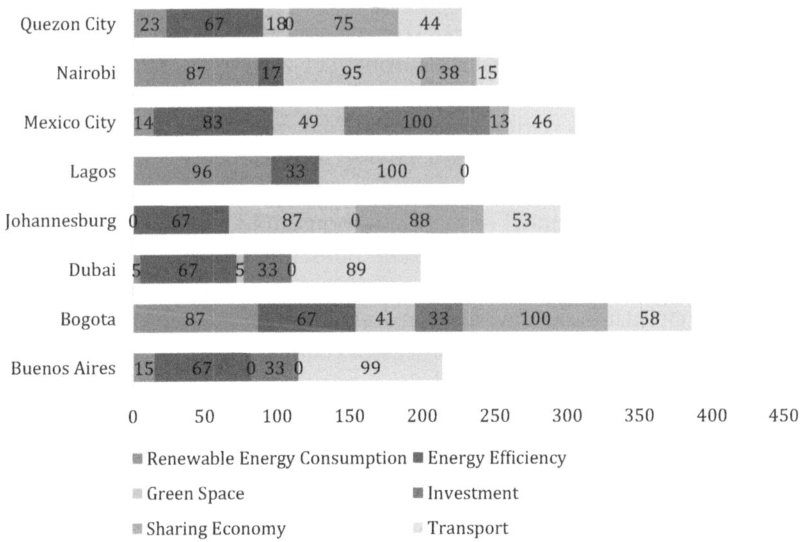

Fig. 1.7 Circular city barometer: energy, ecology, investment, and mobility scores in selected global cities (*Data source* Bloomberg [2025])

Circular strategies address this gap through four core practices: maximisation of product use cycles; substitution of virgin materials with recycled inputs; reduction of material intensity through optimised design; and scaling of recycling infrastructure (World Economic Forum, 2019). For example, increasing the number of use cycles for industrial components reduces the need for new production. Material substitution (e.g., using recycled aluminium) reduces emissions relative to primary material extraction. These practices collectively improve material efficiency, lower emissions, and reduce resource dependency, outcomes essential for emerging economies seeking cost-effective paths to sustainable growth (Khalifa et al., 2022).

Significantly, circular economy principles extend beyond the industrial sectors. Agriculture, water management, and energy systems in emerging markets also benefit from circular practices, such as nutrient recycling, water reuse, and the deployment of decentralised renewable energy (Khalifa et al., 2022). However, challenges still exist. Fragmented supply chains, limited technological capacity, and weak collaboration among firms hinder the implementation of the circular economy, particularly in low-capacity emerging economies (World Economic Forum, 2019).

Emerging markets, while vital to global net-zero goals, face significant financial barriers. Standard Chartered estimates that emerging economies require approximately USD 94.8 trillion in additional investment to complete their transition by 2060 (World Economic Forum, 2022). If forced to self-finance via higher taxation or debt issuance, these countries would face a 5% annual reduction in household consumption, which could potentially exacerbate poverty and hinder economic growth (World Economic Forum, 2022). This financing gap also constrains the adoption of the circular economy; circular infrastructure, recycling industries, and the redesign of production processes require capital investment, yet few emerging economies can fund these transitions independently. Thus, the development of robust domestic capital markets and the mobilisation of FDI represent crucial enablers for circular economy implementation (OECD, 2025).

Despite these obstacles, emerging economies are already contributing to a global circular net-zero. In Brazil, projects such as the Revolusolar supply decentralised solar energy systems in urban communities, combining renewable energy access with resource-efficient infrastructure (World Economic Forum, 2022). In Asia, China dominates global solar photovoltaic (PV) production, whereas Southeast Asian economies lead global battery supply chains, which are critical for electric vehicles (Besedina & Salazar, 2022). These industries exemplify how circular economy-aligned technologies can underpin both decarbonisation and economic development.

Beyond technological investment, behavioural change and ecosystem coordination are necessary to scale circular economy transitions. Khalifa et al. (2022) emphasise that shifting consumer preferences, corporate cultures, and industry practices towards circularity is a core enabler. Multi-stakeholder industrial ecosystems, in which manufacturers, recyclers, designers, and policymakers collaborate, are required to address value chain fragmentation (World Economic Forum, 2019). Policy frameworks and public–private financing mechanisms must reinforce these strategies. The World Economic Forum identifies $83 trillion in private investment opportunities in emerging markets between 2020 and 2060, contingent on effective regulatory environments, carbon pricing instruments, and incentives for circular industries (World Economic Forum, 2022). Directing sustainable finance towards circular economy infrastructure, recycling systems, and material innovation is thus a practical and inclusive route towards net-zero transitions.

1.4 Financing the Transition: Scaling Energy Investment in Emerging Markets

The attainment of global net-zero emissions by 2050 critically depends on energy investment in emerging markets. BloombergNEF (2024) estimates that these low- and middle-income economies must mobilise a cumulative $69 trillion in energy transition capital by mid-century (an average of $2.6 trillion annually) to be on a net-zero path. Such figures represent more than a twofold increase over the average of $1 trillion per year invested since 2020. Without urgent acceleration, these countries will not meet the Paris Agreement's 1.75 °C target and risk entrenchment of carbon-intensive development (BloombergNEF, 2024).

While demand-side systems, such as electric vehicles (EVs) and heat pumps, dominate consumer investment, supply-side transformations must anchor structural shifts in emerging energy systems. These economies need to allocate $0.6 trillion annually to renewables and electricity grid infrastructure, which is five times the historical average for 2020–2023 (BloombergNEF, 2025). Brazil illustrates the role of a favourable policy design. Through rooftop solar incentives and the expansion of wind capacity, the country increased its renewable energy investment by 41% per annum between 2020 and 2023. In contrast, India grew at a slower rate of 20%, and Indonesia experienced a contraction of 20% in the same period, exposing wide regional disparities in the transition momentum (BloombergNEF, 2025).

On the demand side, investment in the energy system must likewise intensify. Emerging markets outside China must invest $1.4 trillion annually through 2050 into demand systems, including $1.2 trillion into EVs alone (BloombergNEF, 2024). These figures reflect not only population and economic growth but also the cost-effectiveness of the electrification of transport fleets. EVs increasingly outperform internal combustion engine (ICE) vehicles in terms of the total cost of ownership, which supports their earlier adoption. Unlike high-income countries, which must scrap ICE vehicles before end-of-life to meet targets (raising transition costs), emerging markets can leapfrog to electric mobility if sufficient capital and infrastructure align (BloombergNEF, 2025).

While emerging markets increased energy transition investment to $1 trillion in 2023 (up 52% from 2020), this accounted for just 14% of the total energy system spending. In contrast, China allocated 49% of its energy investment to low-carbon technologies in the same year, up from 20% in 2020 (BloombergNEF, 2025). This imbalance risks deepening fossil fuel dependency. Under a net-zero scenario, emerging markets must direct 87% of their investment to low-carbon sectors, compared to an even split under a less ambitious economic transition. The latter yields only a 27% emissions reduction and a 2.6 °C global warming trajectory (BloombergNEF, 2024).

Policy design plays a decisive role in shifting these allocations. Governments must go beyond setting renewable targets or declarations of green intention. They need to institutionalise mechanisms such as carbon pricing, auction schemes, vehicle emissions mandates, and fiscal incentives for grid-scale storage and EV adoption. Such interventions must include sunset clauses to avoid market distortion. However, in countries such as India and Indonesia, slow implementation and overly generous concessions delay structural changes (BloombergNEF, 2025). To remain credible, governments must phase out temporary exemptions and rigorously enforce compliance timelines.

Creating a supportive financial environment is critical. Many emerging markets face high capital costs, shallow financial markets, and regulatory uncertainty. Public development banks, multilateral finance institutions, and private capital must collaborate via blended financing, concessional loans, and de-risking instruments. Without these, few projects reach commercial viability. Governments must coordinate industrial policies to ensure capital reaches domestic supply chains and maximises local economic multipliers. Otherwise, global investors may bypass local markets in favour of safer or more predictable alternatives.

Importantly, this investment challenge presents an opportunity for strategic development. The $69 trillion figure should not be framed solely as a cost (BloombergNEF, 2024). Instead, it offers a vehicle for inclusive industrialisation, infrastructure upgrading, and employment generation. Solar manufacturing, EV assembly, and grid digitisation provide long-term economic value and reduce dependence on volatile fossil imports. Provided that complementary policies are in place, early movers will gain a competitive advantage and build resilient green economies.

1.5 Social, Ethical, and Equity Dimensions of Sustainability in Emerging Markets

Sustainability transitions in emerging markets must prioritise social justice, equity, and ethical responsibility. As Avelino et al. (2024) argue, the integration of justice and sustainability is indispensable to the elimination of power asymmetries and the inclusion of marginalised voices in transformation processes. Emerging economies, particularly in Sub-Saharan Africa, Southeast Asia, and Latin America, face compounded structural barriers. These include employment disruptions, digital divides, and ethical risks associated with technology adoption. These issues make it harder for them to transition to net-zero and circular economies. Labour market transformations depict the complexity of sustainability transitions. The World Economic Forum estimates that 170 million new jobs will emerge by 2030, driven by green industries and digital technologies. However, 92 million existing roles will be displaced by automation and structural change, resulting in a net gain of 78 million jobs (IEEE, 2025). OECD (2024) data reveal sharp regional disparities in workforce readiness. While approximately 20% of workers in OECD countries hold jobs with significant "green task" content, this share is as low as 7% in many emerging regions, especially in rural Africa and South Asia. This discrepancy underscores the urgent need for workforce reskilling. Initiatives such as Nigeria's Tech4Dev programme, which has upskilled over 36,000 youths in digital skills, illustrate scalable skills-based approaches (Phillips Consulting, 2024).

Digital exclusion further undermines equitable participation in sustainable economies. Infrastructure deficits and affordability barriers persist across many emerging economies. In Nigeria, the DigiGap initiative expanded internet access among rural youths by subsidisation of connectivity costs (Phillips Consulting, 2024). Nevertheless, informal economies, low digital literacy, and infrastructural inequities in countries such as Ethiopia and Mozambique continue to marginalise large populations from digital climate solutions (IEEE, 2025). Addressing these divides requires policy frameworks that integrate public investment with inclusive digital education strategies.

The deployment of environmental, social, and governance (ESG) technologies has raised significant ethical concerns. In emerging markets, weak data protection laws exacerbate risks of personal data misuse and digital surveillance (Sustainability Directory, 2025). Automation-driven job displacement threatens labour-intensive sectors, potentially exacerbating poverty and social instability if not mitigated through proactive workforce policies (IEEE, 2025). Additionally, environmental justice concerns arise when technological interventions (e.g., waste management innovations) disproportionately benefit formal urban centres while sidelining informal sector workers who sustain critical recycling activities (Reis-Filho et al., 2025).

Avelino et al. (2024) highlight the interplay of politics, power, and prefiguration in shaping justice-oriented transitions. The inclusion of marginalised voices (e.g., informal sector actors, women, and rural populations) within governance processes enhances both equity and transition effectiveness. Grassroots participation, as evidenced by waste-picker cooperatives in Latin American cities, can strengthen circular outcomes while safeguarding livelihoods (Reis-Filho et al., 2025).

Institutional responses must, therefore, adopt inclusion-centric frameworks that address systemic inequalities. This includes formalising the informal sector's contributions, integrating diversity and inclusion (DEI) principles into policy design, and investing in capacity-building (Borg Ellul & Friggieri, 2025). Financial inclusion via mobile-enabled services, as demonstrated in Kenya and India, can facilitate equitable access to digital economic opportunities (United Nations Capital Development Fund, 2013). Equally, environmental justice demands that clean energy access and waste management solutions distribute benefits fairly across the urban–rural and gender divides. Ethically sustainable transitions require multi-scalar strategies that respect local contexts, promote fair labour outcomes, safeguard human rights, as well as support institutional transparency. In resource-constrained environments, as Sharmelly and Ray (2021) argue, frugal and reverse innovations offer pathways for developing context-appropriate technologies that mitigate ethical risks while enabling economic inclusion.

1.6 Methodological Approach: Literature- and Report-Based Analysis

This book adopts a literature- and report-based methodological approach, drawing exclusively on secondary sources to ensure comprehensive and contextually relevant evidence. The evidence base integrates peer-reviewed academic literature, industry reports, and policy papers from leading institutions, such as the OECD (2025), Bloomberg (2025), and the Ellen MacArthur Foundation (Charnley, 2022). This interdisciplinary body of knowledge enables the analysis to synthesise insights from economics, policy, technology, as well as business perspectives relevant to emerging markets.

The approach prioritises context-specific secondary data and case studies. Reports from the African Development Bank (n.d.) and Climate Policy Initiative (Meattle et al., 2024) contribute regionally focused data, while empirical studies addressing circular economy practices in Sub-Saharan Africa (Ruth & El-Amin, 2025) and waste management innovations in Latin America (Bijos et al., 2022) provide operational insights. Country-level case studies, such as Vietnam's green bond markets (Nguyen et al., 2024) and Brazil's national development banks (Green Policy Platform, 2019), enhance geographic specificity.

Reliance on secondary sources has inherent limitations, including the potential absence of granular sector-specific data and variability in data quality across regions. Nevertheless, triangulating institutional reports with the academic literature strengthens the reliability of the findings. The breadth of the evidence base allows for comparative analysis across diverse sectors and countries, highlighting critical patterns and divergences in sustainable development strategies. Overall, this methodological approach provides a robust, interdisciplinary foundation for analysing the intersection of a circular economy and net-zero transitions in emerging markets.

1.7 Theoretical Foundations and Practical Relevance

This book applies three interconnected theoretical frameworks (Institutional Theory, Diffusion of Innovations (DoI) Theory, and the Resource-Based View (RBV)) to examine the circular economy and net-zero transitions in emerging markets. Each framework addresses distinct but interdependent challenges: governance barriers, technology adoption, as well as firm-level capabilities. Collectively, they structure both macro-level and micro-level analyses throughout the book.

Institutional Theory frames the assessment of governance structures, particularly the persistence of institutional voids and enforcement deficits. Emerging markets often face weak regulatory institutions, fragmented policies, alongside limited technical capacities, which constrain formal governance of circular and net-zero transitions (Rweyendela & Kombe, 2021). In Sub-Saharan Africa, informal sector actors (e.g., waste collectors) deliver critical recycling services beyond the scope of formal regulations (Ruth & El-Amin, 2025). This reflects not an absence of governance but a reliance on informal systems shaped by necessity. Institutional Theory posits that coercive, normative, and mimetic pressures (Dragomir et al., 2023) drive sustainability in advanced economies but exert limited influence in contexts where formal institutions lack legitimacy. Consequently, adaptive hybrid governance models that integrate informal actors into formal strategies become essential. This book applies Institutional Theory to recommend governance models that are sensitive to institutional realities in Sub-Saharan Africa, South Asia, and Latin America.

The diffusion of innovation theory (Rogers, 2003) explains how and why technologies supporting a circular economy and net-zero goals disseminate unevenly across emerging markets. Core innovation attributes (e.g., relative advantage, compatibility, complexity, trialability, and observability) determine adoption success. For instance, blockchain-based supply chain solutions face adoption barriers in resource-constrained economies due to perceived complexity and lack of visible benefits (Guan et al., 2023). Conversely, solar-powered microgrids in rural Africa demonstrate high trialability and observable benefits, enabling wider adoption (Amankwah-Amoah & Hinson, 2024). DoI Theory is used to analyse adoption across sectors, such as agriculture, energy, and waste management, and to identify both technology-specific and institutional barriers. The Resource-Based View (RBV) focuses on firm-level capabilities (Barney, 1991), which helps explain why corporate engagement with circular and net-zero strategies is uneven across emerging markets. Firms require valuable, rare, inimitable, and organisationally embedded resources (e.g., advanced emissions-monitoring technologies, climate-aligned finance, skilled personnel, and operational routines) to align with sustainability goals. For example, firms in Southeast Asia leverage AI-enabled carbon accounting (Asuene, 2024), while SMEs in Africa often lack the digital infrastructure and financial resources necessary for emissions reporting (Clean Air Fund, 2022). RBV clarifies that capability deficits, rather than strategic intent alone, limit corporate transitions. This framework guides the book's analysis of how internal resources shape firm strategies in industrial decarbonisation and circular value chains.

Together, these frameworks enable systemic and multi-level analyses of sustainability transitions in emerging markets. Institutional Theory addresses structural governance constraints, the DoI Theory explains the dynamics of technology diffusion, and the RBV captures firm-specific resource limitations. Their integration supports both theoretical depth and practical relevance, informing governance reforms, technology policies, and corporate strategy recommendations throughout the book.

1.8 Structure and Flow of the Book

This book is organised into seven interconnected chapters, each addressing the key dimensions of the circular economy and net-zero transitions in emerging markets. The sequence of chapters reflects progression from technological enablers to corporate strategies, financing mechanisms, sectoral applications, and governance frameworks, culminating in a strategic synthesis.

Chapter 2 explores how digital and disruptive technologies, specifically, artificial intelligence, blockchain, Internet of Things, quantum computing, and digital twins, can facilitate resource efficiency and emissions reduction across emerging markets. Drawing on the Diffusion of Innovations theory and Institutional Theory, the chapter examines the adoption conditions, regional disparities, and institutional voids that hinder technological diffusion. The analysis underscores the strategic importance of regulatory sandboxes, regional cooperation, and public–private partnerships in unlocking the technological potential for circular and net-zero transitions.

Chapter 3 examines corporate strategies for achieving sustainability goals. Using the resource-based view, it assesses how firms' technological, financial, and human resource capacities affect their ability to operationalise circular economy models and achieve credible net-zero commitments. The chapter presents case-based analysis of firms in Sub-Saharan Africa, Southeast Asia, and Latin America, examining practices such as emissions accounting, product redesign, and reverse logistics. Institutional fragility and financing constraints have emerged as key barriers to deeper corporate engagement.

Chapter 4 investigates green financing and investment mechanisms that support sustainability transitions. The chapter evaluates the role of green bonds, sustainability-linked loans, carbon markets, development banks, and regulatory frameworks. It identifies structural constraints within sustainable investment ecosystems and proposes fintech solutions, capacity-building strategies, and regional cooperation to address financing gaps. Chapter 5 examines the sectoral applications in food systems and urban development. The analysis highlights regulatory fragmentation, informality, and socio-cultural barriers that limit circular economy adoption. Drawing on Diffusion of Innovations theory and institutional analysis, it reveals the need for modular technologies and inclusive governance in sectors critical to sustainability transitions.

Chapter 6 analyses policy frameworks and global implications. Institutional Theory frames the examination of governance deficits, informal sector roles, and the need for adaptive, multi-level policies to advance the circular economy and net-zero strategies. Recommendations focus on harmonised standards, participatory governance, and institutional strengthening.

Finally, Chapter 7 synthesises key insights and presents a pragmatic, multi-level roadmap for policy and governance reform. By emphasising institutional legitimacy, informal sector inclusion, and regional cooperation, this book concludes that sustainable transitions demand context-specific, inclusive, and adaptive strategies.

1.9 Conclusion

We conclude that the sustainability challenge in emerging markets is both a crisis and a transformative opportunity. These economies face a triple burden: historical underinvestment, climate vulnerability, and systemic inequality. However, they also possess the demographic, geographic, and resource leverage to reimagine development on more equitable and regenerative terms.

Our exploration reveals that global sustainability solutions must go beyond decarbonisation to integrate circular economy principles, including minimisation of resource extraction, recirculation of materials, and the integration of equity into policy design. Evidence indicates that circular practices not only mitigate emissions but also promote local resilience and inclusive economic growth when supported by robust institutions and financing mechanisms.

Historical carbon debts, unmet climate finance pledges, and regressive policy instruments reinforce global inequities. We emphasise the necessity of international cooperation and justice-based frameworks. Without structural reforms in global trade, finance, and governance, the sustainability transition risks deepening the North–South divide. Moreover, emerging markets are not homogeneous. Institutional capacities, industrial structures, and digital ecosystems have varied widely. Therefore, the one-size-fits-all approach is inadequate. Instead, context-sensitive strategies that empower local actors, bridge informal and formal systems, and invest in workforce readiness are essential.

We believe that aligning the net-zero and circular economy agendas through the lens of institutional theory, innovation diffusion, and firm-level capabilities provides a robust roadmap for change. If supported by inclusive governance, equitable finance, and stakeholder collaboration, emerging markets can become global leaders, not laggards, in sustainability transitions. The path is complex, but the opportunity is historic.

References

Amankwah-Amoah, J., & Hinson, R. E. (2024). Scaling up and scaling out of darkness: Elucidating the influences of institutional dysfunction in scaling up solar PV in Sub-Saharan Africa. *World Development, 183*, Article 106726.

Andaman Partners. (2025). *Who trades with who? A regional breakdown of the global direction of trade*. https://andamanpartners.com/2025/01/a-regional-breakdown-of-global-direction-of-trade/

Asuene. (2024). ESG trends driving change in the energy sector. Asuene Inc. https://asuene.com/us/blog/esg-trends-driving-change-in-the-energy-sector

Avelino, F., et al. (2024). Just sustainability transitions: Politics, power, and prefiguration in transformative change toward justice and sustainability.

Annual Review of Environment and Resources, 49, 519–547. https://doi.org/10.1146/annurev-environ-112321-081722

Barney, J. (1991). Firm resources and sustained competitive advantage. *Journal of Management, 17*(1), 99–120.

Besedina, G., & Salazar, P. (2022, December 23). *Net zero with emerging markets: Before the bell tolls.* https://www.candriam.com/es/professional/insights/highlighted/outlook-2023/net-zero-with-emerging-markets-before-the-bell-tolls/

Bislimi, F., Dalloshi, P., Mehmeti, I., & Deda, G. (2024). Digital readiness in emerging markets: The role of digital skills and connectivity in driving digital economy. *International Journal of Religion, 5*(11), 4316–4324. https://doi.org/10.61707/5ytxj483

Bijos, J. C., Zanta, V. M., Morato, J., Queiroz, L. M., & Oliveira-Esquerre, K. P. (2022). Improving circularity in municipal solid waste management through machine learning in Latin America and the Caribbean. *Sustainable Chemistry and Pharmacy, 28*, 100740.

Bloomberg. (2025). *Circular City Barometer.* https://sponsored.bloomberg.com/immersive/holcim/circular-cities

BloombergNEF. (2024a, November 14). *Net zero hinges on emerging markets outside China more than doubling annual energy investment*. https://about.bnef.com/insights/clean-energy/net-zero-hinges-on-emerging-markets-outside-china-more-than-doubling-annual-energy-investment/

BloombergNEF. (2025b, January 7). *BloombergNEF on the emerging markets net zero challenge*. https://www.bloomberg.com/professional/insights/sustainable-finance/bloombergnef-on-the-emerging-markets-net-zero-challenge/

Borg Ellul, D., & Friggieri, J. (2025). A thriving future through diversity, equity, and inclusion for resilient and innovative communities. *IntechOpen*. https://doi.org/10.5772/intechopen.1008368

Charnley, F. (2022, June 14). *The circular economy: Towards net zero.* UK Research and Innovation. https://www.ukri.org/blog/the-circular-economy-towards-net-zero/

Clean Air Fund. (2022). *The state of global air quality funding 2022.* Clean Air Fund. https://www.cleanairfund.org/air-quality-funding-2022/

Dragomir, V. D., Dumitru, M., & Perevoznic, F. M. (2023). Carbon reduction and energy transition targets of the largest European companies: An empirical study based on institutional theory. *Cleaner Production Letters, 4*, 100039.

Environmental Justice Foundation. (2022). *Inequality is worsening as climate crisis deepens*. https://ejfoundation.org/news-media/inequality-is-worsening-as-climate-crisis-deepens-new-report

Feffer, J. (2025, March 27). *The growing inequality among countries and the worsening climate crisis*. The Observatory. https://www.resilience.org/stories/2025-03-27/the-growing-inequality-among-countries-and-the-worsening-climate-crisis/

Fragkos, P. (2022). Analysing the systemic implications of energy efficiency and circular economy strategies in the decarbonisation context. *AIMS Energy, 10*(2), 191–218. https://doi.org/10.3934/energy.2022011

Green Policy Platform. (2019). *Financing Climate Futures: The role of National Development Banks in Brazil and South Africa*. Global Green Growth Institute / Green Policy Platform. https://www.greenfinanceplatform.org/case-studies/financing-climate-futures-role-national-development-banks-brazil-and-south-africa

Grynspan, R. (2025, January 7). *For a more just global economy: The role of Latin America*. UN Trade and Development (UNCTAD). https://unctad.org/news/more-just-global-economy-role-latin-america

Guan, W., Ding, W., Zhang, B., & Verny, J. (2023). The role of supply chain alignment in coping with resource dependency in blockchain adoption: empirical evidence from China. *Journal of enterprise information management, 36*(2), 605–628.

Hachileka, E. (2025, July 16). *Turning carbon into opportunity: How Africa's carbon markets can power people and deliver the SDGs*. UNDP Africa. https://www.undp.org/africa/blog/turning-carbon-opportunity-how-africas-carbon-markets-can-power-people-and-deliver-sdgs

Hailemariam, A., & Erdiaw-Kwasie, M. O. (2022). Towards a circular economy: Implications for emission reduction and environmental sustainability. *Business Strategy and the Environment, 32*(4), 1951–1965. https://doi.org/10.1002/bse.3229

Hassan, H., & Faggian, R. (2023). System thinking approaches for circular economy: Enabling inclusive, synergistic, and eco-effective pathways for sustainable development. *Frontiers in Sustainability, 4*, Article 1267282. https://doi.org/10.3389/frsus.2023.1267282

IEEE. (2025, June 30). *Re-skilling for a sustainable, digital future*. https://sustainable-climate.ieee.org/news/reskilling-for-sustainable-digital-future/

Integral Consult. (2021). *Needs of African countries related to implementing the UN Framework Convention on Climate Change and the Paris Agreement*. https://unfccc.int/sites/default/files/resource/Needs%20Report_African%20counties_AfDB_FINAL.pdf

Karlin, A., & Sierra-Escalante, K. (2021). *Blended concessional finance: The benefits of transparency and access* (EMCompass Note No. 105). International Finance Corporation. https://openknowledge.worldbank.org/entities/publication/10b37399-1051-5bf8-8200-345aef581f47

Khalifa, A. A., Ibrahim, A.-J., Amhamed, A. I., & El-Naas, M. H. (2022). Accelerating the transition to a circular economy for net-zero emissions by 2050: A systematic review. *Sustainability, 14*(18), 11656. https://doi.org/10.3390/su141811656

Law, Y. K., & Fong, C. S. (2025). Emerging markets' carbon pricing development: A comparative analysis of China and South Korea's experience. *World, 6*(2), 58. https://doi.org/10.3390/world6020058

Lazzaro, N. (2025, June 9). Emerging markets in Asia, Latin America attract investors amid trade tensions. *S&P Global Market Intelligence*. https://www.spglobal.com/market-intelligence/en/news-insights/articles/2025/6/emerging-markets-in-asia-latin-america-attract-investors-amid-trade-tensions-89974745

Legal Response International. (2022). *Carbon trading schemes around the world*. https://legalresponse.org/legaladvice/carbon-trading-schemes-around-the-world/

Mammadov, K. (2025, April 14). *Emerging markets face a perfect storm*. IMF PFM Blog. https://blog-pfm.imf.org/en/pfmblog/2025/04/emerging-markets-face-a-perfect-storm

Meattle, C., Balm, A., Diaz, J. E., Miao, G., Stout, S., Gupta, I., Abraham, S., Sloley, A., & Wignarajah, D. (2024). Landscape of climate finance in Africa 2024. *Climate Policy Initiative*. https://www.climatepolicyinitiative.org/publication/landscape-of-climate-finance-in-africa-2024/

Nguyen, P.-H., Nguyen, L.-A. T., Le, H. Q., & Tran, L.-C. (2024). Navigating critical barriers for green bond markets using a fuzzy multi-criteria decision-making model: Case study in Vietnam. *Heliyon, 10*(13), Article e33493. https://doi.org/10.1016/j.heliyon.2024.e33493

OECD. (2024). *OECD Employment Outlook 2024: The net-zero transition and the labour market. OECD Publishing*. https://doi.org/10.1787/ac8b3538-en

OECD. (2025, June 30). *Supporting emerging markets and developing economies in developing their local capital markets: Full report*. https://www.oecd.org/en/publications/supporting-emerging-markets-and-developing-economies-in-developing-their-local-capital-markets_4456de62-en/full-report.html

Pande, R. (2023). The climate crisis is a crisis of inequality. *Science, 381*(6661). https://doi.org/10.1126/science.adk3500

Phillips Consulting. (2024, September 23). *Digital inclusion and equity: Strategies to bridge the digital divide for a sustainable future*. https://proshare.co/articles/digital-inclusion-and-equity-strategies-to-bridge-the-digital-divide-for-a-sustainable-future

Rao, A. (2025). *India's Foreign Direct Investment Tracker 2025*. https://www.india-briefing.com/news/india-fdi-tracker-2025-38140.html/

Reis-Filho, J. A., et al. (2025). Invisible Green Guardians: A long-term study on informal waste pickers' contributions to recycling and the mitigation of greenhouse gas emissions. *Cleaner Waste Systems, 10*, Article 100217. https://doi.org/10.1016/j.clwas.2025.100217

Rogers, E. M. (2003). Diffusion of innovations (5th ed.). Free Press.

Ruth, C., & El-Amin, N. (2025). *Integrating Circular Economy Principles in Developing Economies: Challenges and Opportunities for Sub-Saharan Africa.* https://www.researchgate.net/publication/390771658_Integrating_Circular_Economy_Principles_in_Developing_Economies_Challenges_and_Opportunities_for_Sub-Saharan_Africa

Rweyendela, A. G., & Kombe, G. G. (2021). Institutional influences on circular economy: A Tanzanian perspective. *Sustainable Production and Consumption, 26*, 1062–1073.

Sharmelly, R., & Ray, P. K. (2021). Managing resource-constrained innovation in emerging markets: perspectives from a business model. *Technology in Society, 65*, 101538. https://doi.org/10.1016/j.techsoc.2021.101538

Stripe. (2025). *Emerging markets: A guide to trends, risks, and opportunities.* https://stripe.com/at/resources/more/emerging-markets

Sustainability Directory. (2025). *What are the ethical considerations surrounding ESG technology implementation in emerging markets?* https://sustainability-directory.com/question/what-are-the-ethical-considerations-surrounding-esg-technology-implementation-in-emerging-markets/

Tansan, B., Lang, N., Meyer, M., Gökbulut, A., Ivers, L., Hutchinson, R., Santamarta, S., Azevedo, D., & Chan, T. (2023, March 14). *The sustainability imperative in emerging markets.* Boston Consulting Group. https://www.bcg.com/publications/2023/the-importance-of-sustainability-in-business

United Nations Capital Development Fund. (2013). *Achieving financial inclusion with ICTs.* https://capacity4dev.europa.eu/groups/disability-and-development-network/info/edd2013-thematic-programme-inclusiveness-equity-social-protection_en

World Bank. (2021). *ICP 2021: Size of economies.* https://www.worldbank.org/en/programs/icp/brief/ICP2021_DataViz_1

World Bank. (2023). *How developing countries can measure exposure to the EU's carbon border adjustment mechanism.* https://blogs.worldbank.org/en/trade/how-developing-countries-can-measure-exposure-eus-carbon-border-adjustment-mechanism

World Bank. (2024, January 18). *Digital transformation drives development in Africa.* https://www.worldbank.org/en/results/2024/01/18/digital-transformation-drives-development-in-afe-afw-africa

World Bank. (2025). *World Development Indicators.* http://databank.worldbank.org/data/reports.aspx?source=world-development-indicators

World Economic Forum. (2019). *Circular economy for net-zero industry transition.* https://exeterce.org/knowledge-hub/circular-economy-for-net-zero-industry-transition/

World Economic Forum. (2022, April 5). *Here's why developed economies must bear the $100 trillion cost of the net-zero transition in emerging markets*. https://www.weforum.org/stories/2022/04/emerging-developed-economies-net-zero-transition/

World Inequality Lab. (2023). *Climate inequality report 2023*. Global Research Programme on Inequality (GRIP). https://wid.world/www-site/uploads/2023/01/CBV2023-ClimateInequalityReport-2.pdf

CHAPTER 2

Digital and Disruptive Technologies for Net-Zero and Circularity in Emerging Markets

Abstract In this chapter, we examine the role of digital technologies in accelerating circular economy transitions and enabling net-zero development in emerging markets. We apply *Diffusion of Innovations* (DoI) theory and *institutional theory* to evaluate adoption conditions for key digital tools: artificial intelligence (AI), blockchain, Internet of Things, quantum computing, and digital twins. While these technologies offer significant potential for real-time monitoring, resource efficiency, and climate adaptation, their diffusion remains constrained by infrastructure deficits, regulatory gaps, and limited digital literacy. Our comparative typology assesses relative advantages, feasibility, and governance dependencies. We highlight institutional voids and regional disparities, particularly across Sub-Saharan Africa, Southeast Asia, and Latin America. To address these gaps, we propose inclusive strategies, such as national digital circular economy strategies, regulatory sandboxes, green public procurement, development finance, and public–private partnerships.

Keywords Digital technologies · Circular economy · Net-Zero transition · Emerging markets · Artificial Intelligence (AI) · Blockchain · Institutional theory · Diffusion of innovations · Resource-based view (RBV)

O. Evans and O. Adeola, *Innovations in Circular Economy and Net Zero*, https://doi.org/10.1007/978-3-032-22094-3_2

2.1 Introduction

The climate crisis has heightened the urgency for countries, especially those in emerging markets, to pursue development models that decouple growth from carbon intensity and resource waste. As the Paris Agreement and the Sustainable Development Goals (SDGs) establish clear global mandates for climate neutrality and circularity, emerging economies face the dual challenge of sustaining economic expansion while reducing ecological and material footprints (Lee, 2023). Digital technology is a vital tool in accelerating this shift. When designed for system-wide transformation, digital tools such as artificial intelligence, blockchain, Internet of Things (IoT), and digital twins can reconfigure extractive, linear infrastructures into regenerative, circular models. These technologies enable real-time monitoring, enhance transparency, and support predictive and lifecycle-based resource management (Hariyani et al., 2024; Rejeb et al., 2022).

Recent trends in digital infrastructure and connectivity across emerging markets indicate an encouraging trajectory for digital readiness, with clear implications for accelerating the circular economy and facilitating net-zero transitions (Fig. 2.1). Between 2015 and 2022, Internet usage surged in countries such as India (from 14.9% to 55.9%), Vietnam (from 45% to 78.6%), and Indonesia (from 22.1% to 66.5%), indicating widespread gains in digital access (World Bank, 2024). Secure internet server deployment expanded exponentially, with South Africa registering a nearly 56-fold increase, and Argentina, Vietnam, and Brazil each recording more than 40-fold growth, underscoring the digital backbone required for advanced applications such as blockchain and data sharing. Mobile cellular subscription is strong across the board, with Colombia, Kenya, and Vietnam exceeding 120 subscriptions per 100 people in 2022, highlighting pervasive mobile connectivity as a key delivery mechanism for digital services. While high-technology export shares declined in some economies, Vietnam and Mexico demonstrated resilience and growth, maintaining export profiles above 20%, suggesting a foothold in the globally competitive technology sectors. Collectively, these indicators reflect substantial digital momentum and a growing capacity to support technology-led sustainability transitions.

In this chapter, we build on recent advances in digital infrastructure to examine how climate- and circularity-aligned digital technologies (e.g., AI, IoT, blockchain, and digital twins) can diffuse across emerging

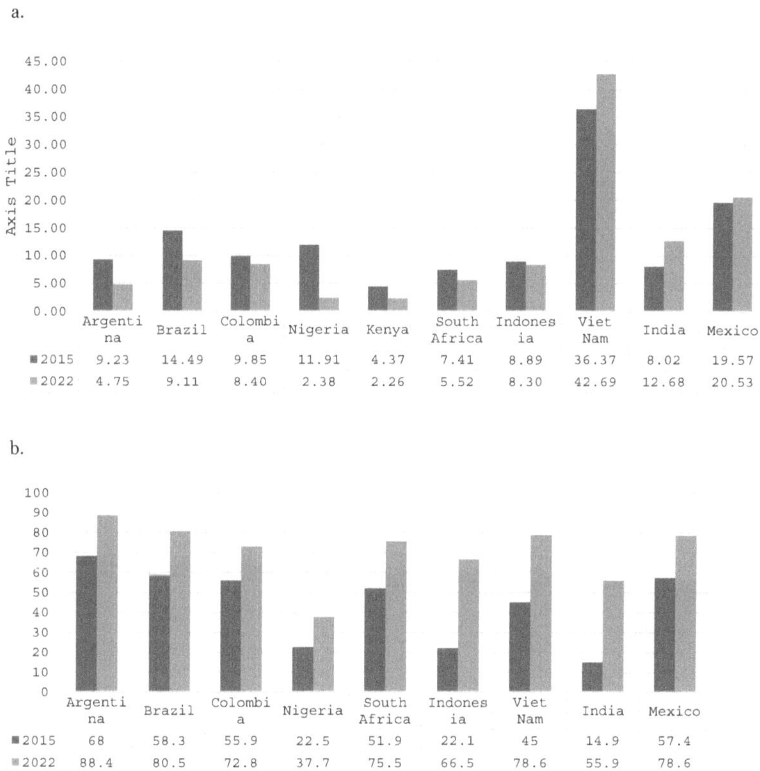

Fig. 2.1 Recent trends in digital infrastructure and connectivity across emerging markets. **a** High-technology exports (% of manufactured exports). **b** Individuals using the Internet (% of population). **c** Mobile cellular subscriptions (per 100 people). **d**. Secure Internet servers (per 1 million people) (*Data source* World Development Indicators [2025])

markets. We apply the DoI (Rogers, 2003) and Institutional Theory to investigate three central questions: Who adopts these technologies? How rapidly can they scale? Under what institutional, infrastructural, and socio-political conditions do they thrive? These questions are especially critical in settings where access to bandwidth, digital literacy, and regulatory readiness are uneven. Yet, technological leapfrogging and mobile-first

c.

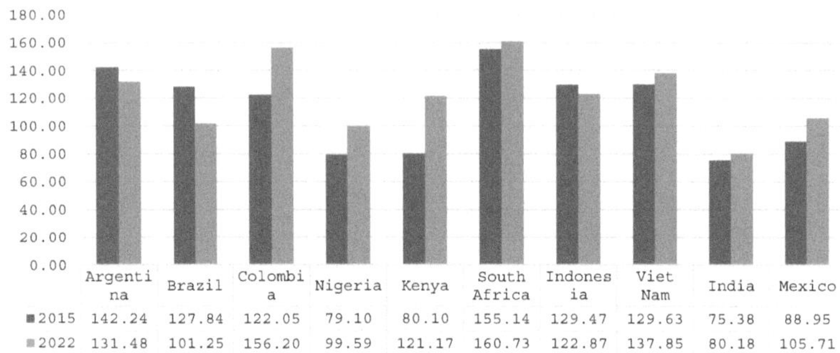

d.

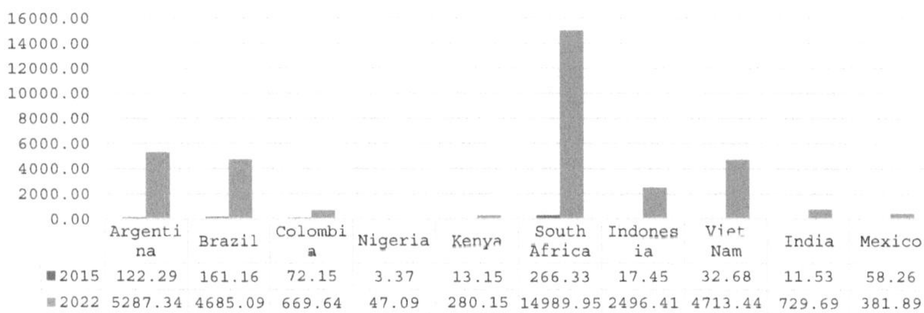

Fig. 2.1 (continued)

solutions present significant opportunities to align digital uptake with sustainability transitions.

2.2 Theoretical Anchors: Understanding Adoption in Climate and Circular Transitions

The effective dissemination of climate-smart and circular innovations in emerging markets requires theoretical tools that account for both innovation characteristics and the institutional environments that shape their uptake. We apply the diffusion of innovations theory and institutional theory to explain why some climate and circular technologies scale, while others stagnate, particularly in low- and middle-income countries.

2.2.1 Diffusion of Innovations (DoI) Theory

Rogers (2003) developed the DoI theory to explain how new ideas and technologies spread across populations. This theory identifies five core attributes (relative advantage, compatibility, complexity, trialability, and observability) that influence an innovation's adoption rate (see Table 2.1). These attributes directly affect the viability of climate-related and circular innovations. For example, solar-powered microgrids offer a high relative advantage and moderate trialability compared to diesel systems, which facilitates their growing deployment across Africa (Amankwah-Amoah & Hinson, 2024). Likewise, waste-tracking platforms tend to succeed in urban municipalities when decision makers perceive compatibility with existing regulatory systems and observe tangible performance outcomes (Izuchukwu et al., 2025).

DoI theory categorises adopters into five sequential segments (innovators, early adopters, early majority, late majority, and laggards), which align clearly with the uptake dynamics of digital agriculture technologies across sub-Saharan Africa (Choruma et al., 2024). Empirical evidence suggests that early adopters often include mobile-enabled smallholder farmers who use simple, accessible tools such as mobile money, SMS-based weather forecasts, and phone-based advisory services. These technologies require only basic digital capacity and offer tangible benefits, including improved market access, income generation, and enhanced farm management decision-making (Choruma et al., 2024). For instance, the iCow platform in Kenya has enabled early adopters to increase both

Table 2.1 Core attributes of diffusion of innovations and their application to circular/climate technologies

Attribute (DoI theory)	*Definition*	*Climate/circular example*
Relative Advantage	Perceived superiority over alternatives	Solar microgrids vs. diesel systems
Compatibility	Fit with existing values, systems	Waste-tracking aligning with regulations
Complexity	Ease of understanding and use	Blockchain-based platforms seen as complex
Trialability	Opportunity to experiment	Mobile apps piloted by cooperatives
Observability	Visible outcomes and benefits	Municipal waste tech with public dashboards

productivity and livestock income, while AgroTech Smartex has helped farmers attract large-scale produce buyers by improving credit access and record-keeping (Choruma et al., 2024). Similarly, mobile money users in Uganda and Kenya have reported better market integration and profitability compared to non-users. These adoption patterns reflect the influence of DoI factors such as relative advantage, trialability, and observability in shaping diffusion. However, Choruma et al. (2024) also identified structural barriers that limit progression into later adopter categories (e.g., low digital literacy, limited infrastructure, and inadequate training), particularly among women and older farmers.

2.2.2 *Institutional Theory*

Institutional Theory complements DoI by focusing on systemic rules, norms, and beliefs that influence how and whether innovation diffuses. Scott (2008) defined institutions across three pillars: regulative structures (laws, standards), normative frameworks (social expectations), and cognitive schemas (shared understandings) (see Table 2.2). These elements collectively determine the capacity and legitimacy of innovation. In climate transitions, institutions shape what constitutes "valid" environmental action and influence the resource flows required for adoption.

Empirical evidence from Ethiopia illustrates how institutional fragmentation constrains climate innovation (Matewos, 2019). Although federal policies on climate adaptation exist, Matewos (2019, p. 47) revealed weak coordination among institutions working on climate change adaptation: "As a result, climate adaptation policy implementation lacks continuity, monitoring, and evaluation systems, and fails to yield transformative

Table 2.2 Institutional theory pillars and barriers to circular/climate tech adoption

Institutional pillar	*Definition*	*Barrier example*
Regulative	Laws, policies, standards	Weak or unclear environmental regulation
Normative	Social norms and values	Low public support without trusted actors
Cognitive	Shared beliefs and understandings	Misalignment with informal economies

changes to the farmers". These institutional weaknesses limit the success of decentralised interventions such as circular farming practices, which require monitoring, community participation, and sustained institutional support.

Consumer responses also reflect the institutional context. Godefroit-Winkel (2023) demonstrated that institutional credibility has a significant influence on public acceptance of climate interventions. In Morocco, consumers showed stronger support for climate initiatives led by national or local businesses, whereas French respondents preferred corporate-led actions over state programs (Godefroit-Winkel, 2023). These findings suggest that actor legitimacy (whether public or private) directly influences the perceived trustworthiness and viability of sustainability innovations.

Institutional fragility continues to hinder adoption in many emerging economies (Godefroit-Winkel, 2023; Matewos, 2019). Policymakers often fail to implement carbon pricing or circular economy standards due to resource constraints or political resistance. Informal systems, such as unregulated recycling, operate outside institutional oversight, making it difficult to formalise or integrate into circular transitions (Awasthi et al., 2016). Without deliberate institutional scaffolding (e.g., policy clarity, regulatory sandboxes, green procurement schemes, and investment in climate governance), digital technologies for circularity and net-zero will struggle to scale equitably.

2.3 Core Digital Technologies and Their Circular/Net-Zero Diffusion Potential

The ability of digital technologies to accelerate circular economy outcomes and net-zero targets depends not only on their functionality but also on their adoption, integration, and governance, particularly in emerging markets. This section assesses Artificial Intelligence (AI), Blockchain, Internet of Things (IoT), sensor networks, quantum computing, and big data and digital twins as enablers of circularity and decarbonisation. This analysis is framed within the context of DoI theory and Institutional Theory, with a focus on adoption dynamics, regulatory ecosystems, and emerging market cases.

2.3.1 *Artificial Intelligence (AI)*

AI plays a catalytic role in circular and net-zero transitions by enabling system-level optimisation, emissions prediction, and adaptive climate modelling. In energy systems, AI supports predictive maintenance and load forecasting, improves operational efficiency, and reduces carbon intensity (Li et al., 2024). In agriculture, AI facilitates climate-resilient cropping decisions and smart irrigation. AI also strengthens waste analytics by forecasting collection routes and improving sorting outcomes in urban circular systems (Olawade et al., 2024).

AI applications increasingly emerge in developing economies, albeit unevenly. In India, the *Responsible AI for Social Empowerment (RAISE)* initiative aims to integrate AI into public service delivery (Elbashir & Desikachari, 2025), including agriculture and climate resilience. In Kenya, *Twiga Foods* leverages AI to optimise food logistics and reduce post-harvest waste (Business Tech Africa, 2025), thereby directly contributing to emissions reduction. In Indonesia, the waste management company Tridi Oasis employs AI-powered systems to sort waste at its recycling plants (Brahim & Lahiani, 2025). Mondal et al. (2024)found that AI strategies aligned with digital inclusion, data infrastructure, and stakeholder coordination significantly improved carbon neutrality outcomes in Vietnam and Malaysia.

From a DoI perspective, AI demonstrates high relative advantage and strong observability, particularly through highly visible pilots in smart cities and precision agriculture. However, trialability remains limited in many rural and informal contexts due to high entry costs and infrastructure dependence. Adoption tends to concentrate among early adopters within high-capacity institutions or private firms. Meanwhile, low digital literacy and fragmented data ecosystems impede progress towards the early majority, particularly in emerging markets.

Institutionally, the challenges persist. Mondal et al. (2024) identified governance gaps in ethical standards, model transparency, and training data equity. While national AI strategies exist in India, Rwanda, and Ghana, few offer enforceable guidelines on energy efficiency, open access, or algorithmic accountability. The energy footprint of AI infrastructure (particularly in training large models) raises concerns in countries reliant on fossil-fuel-based grids. However, SYSTEMIQ (2023) found that when targeted towards high-emission sectors such as power and food systems, AI offers a net positive climate impact, outweighing its operational emissions.

2.3.2 *Blockchain*

Blockchain enables decentralised, verifiable systems that support supply chain transparency, material tracking, and peer-to-peer energy trading (Pakseresht et al., 2022). In climate governance, blockchain underpins carbon credit traceability and validates emissions offsets. In circular systems, it supports waste flow accountability, e-waste provenance, as well as product lifecycle mapping, offering new tools to reduce information asymmetry (Pakseresht et al., 2022).

Emerging markets are demonstrating blockchain innovation within the agri-food, waste management, and energy sectors (see Tang et al., 2024). For instance, Kenya is collaborating with the multinational technology corporation IBM on a blockchain initiative designed to allow Kenyans to verify the organic status of their food purchases and ascertain the duration of its market presence (TheCryptoQueen, 2018). In Southeast Asia, the TGO, in conjunction with six green network partners, has initiated an E-Waste ecosystem utilising blockchain technology on the E-Waste+ platform, thereby advancing environmental sustainability (Advanced Info Service, n.d.). Despite their potential, these systems remain at a pilot scale and are insufficiently integrated with national regulatory frameworks.

From a DoI standpoint, blockchain offers a high relative advantage in trust-building and traceability but scores low on trialability and complexity, particularly in low-capacity settings. Adoption is still largely within the innovator and early adopter cohorts (e.g., fintech start-ups or donor-backed sustainability pilots). Broader adoption falters due to technological abstraction, energy intensity, as well as low demonstrability in informal economies. Institutionally, blockchain diffusion confronts several frictions. Balci and Ali (2024) observed that adoption hinges on supply chain information processing capacity, which many developing contexts lack. Regulatory ecosystems are often silent or ambiguous regarding the legal status of blockchain, which limits its integration with formal climate finance and procurement. Few countries (e.g., Rwanda, the Philippines, and Brazil) have introduced blockchain-specific sandboxes or token regulations aligned with green goals.

Furthermore, the blockchain's energy consumption, particularly in proof-of-work protocols, poses a climate paradox unless offset by high-value emissions reductions. SYSTEMIQ (2023) suggested that proof-of-stake and hybrid ledgers offer lower-c alternatives that are more suited to emerging market grids. Without interoperability standards, institutional legitimacy, and capacity-building mechanisms, blockchain will remain a fragmented tool rather than a scalable enabler of circularity and net-zero transitions.

2.3.3 Internet of Things (IoT) and Sensor Networks

The Internet of Things (IoT) enhances climate-neutral and circular systems by enabling real-time monitoring and automation across physical infrastructure. IoT systems optimise energy, water, and waste flows via interconnected sensors and analytics platforms. In agriculture, sensor networks support precision irrigation and soil management, thereby reducing water stress and chemical runoff. In turn, smart grids use IoT-enabled feedback to balance loads and reduce energy losses (Maksimovic, 2017).

In urban environments, the IoT underpins smart city loops (e.g., waste sorting, adaptive lighting, and decentralised energy exchanges). Rejeb et al. (2022)found that IoT directly supports circular economy principles (e.g., reuse, recovery, and recycling), provided that integration occurs across multiple nodes. IoT aligns well with the DoI theory through its high observability and technical compatibility with existing monitoring systems.

Nevertheless, diffusion remains constrained. High capital expenditure, inconsistent rural connectivity, and a lack of interoperability standards weaken adoption, especially in fragmented governance contexts obtainable in emerging contexts. Adamidis et al. (n.d.) argued that scalable IoT-circularity models require coherent digital ecosystems, including power-efficient hardware, open data standards, and institutional frameworks for security and system integrity. Without investment in decentralised infrastructure and regulatory coordination, IoT will be confined to isolated pilots rather than broad-based, climate-aligned transformations in emerging markets.

2.3.4 *Quantum Computing*

Quantum computing has the theoretical potential to revolutionise circularity and climate modelling through unprecedented data-processing capabilities. As technology is still in the early stages of development, quantum systems could enable closed-loop material flow simulations, low-energy system optimisation, as well as climate risk analytics beyond classical computational thresholds (Ali et al., 2025). In principle, quantum computing can accelerate the decarbonisation of sectors such as logistics, materials science, and clean energy systems through exponentially faster scenario modelling.

However, quantum computing is still largely inaccessible and non-triable, particularly in low-resource environments. As the DoI theory suggests, low trialability and observability hinder its diffusion. Demonstration projects are still rare, and most governments lack the technical capacity or infrastructure to experiment with quantum algorithms in public policy settings. The energy footprint of quantum systems also remains uncertain and could become problematic if not managed through the integration of renewable energy sources.

Therefore, institutional support is critical. Emerging economies aiming to advance climate-aligned quantum applications must invest in public R&D, support sandbox environments, and facilitate translational research partnerships. As Tan (2024) noted, Asian governments increasingly recognise the long-term relevance of emerging technologies, such as quantum computing, in engineering sustainability, but still lack a coherent industrial policy to embed them into decarbonisation pathways. Until such ecosystems mature, quantum computing will remain a high-potential, but low-penetration technology.

2.3.5 *Big Data and Digital Twins*

Big data analytics and digital twins enable the modelling of dynamic, circular systems and the optimisation of net-zero transitions. Digital twins simulate urban energy flows, building lifecycles, and mobility systems in real time. These tools support decision-making regarding material reuse, emissions tracking, and infrastructure adaptation (Meng et al., 2023). In construction, for example, lifecycle-based digital twin systems optimise demolition processes to reduce waste and salvage high-value materials.

Big data directly contributes to circularity by generating system-wide insights into material intensity, embedded emissions, and potential intervention points. Rejeb et al. (2022) found that big data, when integrated with IoT and lifecycle analytics, forms a critical foundation for the operationalisation of circular business models. Further, Ali et al. (2025) demonstrated that digital twins, when aligned with sustainability goals, can serve as decision-making infrastructure to support climate-smart cities.

The DoI attributes of high compatibility and observability make digital twins well-positioned for diffusion, particularly in middle-income countries with existing digital infrastructure. However, privacy concerns, fragmented data ecosystems, and a lack of open data standards limit scalability. Adamidis et al. (n.d.) emphasised the need for robust data governance, inter-agency coordination, and investment in simulation platforms that enable actors across sectors to align planning with sustainability metrics. Without sustained public investment and regulatory innovation, digital twin deployment will likely remain elite and urban-centric. To scale equitably, governments must ensure that open-access models and privacy-respecting platforms underpin the digital twin infrastructure of future circular systems.

2.4 Comparative Typology: Evaluating Technologies for Circular/Climate Transitions in Emerging Markets

Emerging markets have unique opportunities and challenges for the diffusion of digital technologies that support circularity and net-zero transitions. These contexts are often characterised by institutional asymmetry and infrastructure gaps, alongside overlapping informal systems. The ability of digital innovations to deliver climate-smart and resource-efficient outcomes depends not only on technical performance but also on their compatibility with governance systems, affordability, as well as ease of deployment. Table 2.3 presents a comparative typology of the five core digital technologies using the synthesis of Rogers' (2003) DoI criteria and institutional considerations.

Artificial intelligence (AI) possesses a significant advantage in achieving net-zero emissions due to its extensive applicability across various sectors.

Table 2.3 Comparative typology of core digital technologies for circular and net-zero transitions

Technology	*Relative advantage*	*Compatibility*	*Complexity*	*Trialability*	*Observability*	*Infrastructure demand*	*Governance dependency*	*Primary circular/ net-zero role*
Artificial Intelligence (AI)	High	Medium	Medium	Medium	High	High	High	Energy optimisation, predictive waste and crop modelling
Blockchain	High	Low–Medium	High	Low	Medium	Medium	Very High	Carbon traceability, decentralised circular supply chains
IoT & Sensor Networks	High	High	Medium	Medium	High	Very High	Medium	Real-time resource tracking, precision agriculture

(continued)

Table 2.3 (continued)

Technology	*Relative advantage*	*Compatibility*	*Complexity*	*Trialability*	*Observability*	*Infrastructure demand*	*Governance dependency*	*Primary circular/ net-zero role*
Quantum Computing	Very High (theoretical)	Low	Very High	Very Low	Very Low	Extremely High	Very High	Material flow simulation, climate system optimisation
Big Data & Digital Twins	High	High	Medium	High	High	High	Medium–High	Lifecycle emissions tracking, circular city simulation

Note Relative Advantage reflects the perceived value addition towards circularity/net-zero outcomes. Trialability and Observability are particularly critical for diffusion in emerging markets, where pilot and demonstration effects play important roles. Governance Dependency indicates a reliance on formal legal, ethical, and interoperability frameworks

Its high observability and moderate complexity render it particularly suitable for implementation in urban areas equipped with reliable digital infrastructure. Conversely, in rural and under-resourced regions, the diffusion of AI is impeded by the high costs associated with data acquisition, limited trialability, and algorithmic opacity. Nonetheless, countries such as India and Vietnam have responded by formulating national AI strategies that integrate green innovation with inclusive digital literacy (Elbashir & Desikachari, 2025; Mondal et al., 2024).

Blockchain technology offers substantial value for trust-based circular supply chains and carbon traceability. Its decentralised nature is particularly appealing in contexts where institutional trust is deficient. However, blockchain is characterised by high complexity, low trialability, and significant dependency on governance structures. In emerging markets, the adoption of blockchain remains largely limited to pilot initiatives, such as food-tracking systems in Kenya (TheCryptoQueen, 2018) and blockchain-enabled e-waste ecosystems in Southeast Asia (Advanced Info Service, n.d.). In the absence of regulatory sandboxes or decentralised legal frameworks, widespread adoption remains challenging.

The Internet of Things (IoT) and sensor networks demonstrate excellent technical compatibility and observability, making them highly effective for the real-time monitoring of environmental and resource systems. However, their diffusion remains heavily dependent on infrastructure readiness, particularly rural internet coverage, power supply reliability, and sensor maintenance ecosystems. As Maksimovic (2017) and Rejeb et al. (2022) noted, policy frameworks that promote open standards and modular interoperability significantly enhance IoT scalability in emerging economies.

Quantum computing, while extremely promising for climate modelling and closed-loop simulations, currently lacks trialability, observability, plus policy integration in most emerging countries. Its infrastructure needs far exceed what is feasible outside of advanced research clusters. Tan (2024) argues that governments must treat quantum as a strategic horizon technology, best supported through public R&D consortia and regional collaboration, alongside sandbox experimentation with sustainability-oriented use cases.

Big Data and Digital Twins occupy the middle ground between feasibility and sophistication. Their high compatibility, observability, and ability to model urban resilience and infrastructure circularity make them particularly effective in emerging cities with expanding digital backbones. However, diffusion often stalls due to fragmented data ecosystems, poor governance of data ownership, as well as limited capacity to interpret high-volume datasets (Ali et al., 2025; Meng et al., 2023). Open data policies, alongside public–private partnerships to develop simulation platforms, offer a viable path to scaling.

While no single technology is a universal solution, some (e.g., AI, IoT, Digital Twins) exhibit stronger alignment with near-term circularity and net-zero goals in emerging markets. Others (e.g., blockchain and quantum computing) hold long-term promise, but require significant institutional scaffolding before full diffusion becomes viable. Therefore, policymakers must tailor digital technology strategies to local capacity, regulatory maturity, and sustainability priorities.

2.5 Diffusion Challenges in Emerging Markets for Circular and Climate Tech

Digital technologies hold significant promise for advancing climate mitigation and circular transitions. However, in emerging markets, their diffusion often stagnates due to structural, institutional, and socio-cultural bottlenecks. These constraints impede not only access to technology but also the social and institutional structures necessary for transformative change. Understanding these diffusion failures requires a close examination of demand- and supply-side barriers, along with contextual insights from key regions.

A central challenge is the absence of early adopters and innovation champions in the climate-aligned sectors. Smallholder farmers, micro-enterprises, and rural municipalities often perceive digital circular technologies as risky, unfamiliar, or misaligned with short-term priorities. Suresh et al. (2025) found that in Tamil Nadu, India, local intermediaries (e.g., change agents, extension workers) significantly influenced the adoption of digital climate-smart agricultural practices. Where such agents are absent, adoption declines significantly. This indicates that diffusion depends not merely on technological access but also on relational trust, localised communication, as well as intermediary support structures.

Infrastructure voids constitute a second major barrier. Large areas of Sub-Saharan Africa and South Asia lack stable electricity, reliable mobile connectivity, and scalable data storage. Chapungu et al. (2024) noted that, although rural Southern Africa possesses strong community resilience norms, these communities cannot fully exploit AI or IoT solutions due to inadequate power infrastructure and data systems. Similarly, in the CWANA (Central and West Asia and North Africa) region, Tabe-Ojong et al. (2024) highlighted persistent internet fragmentation and power instability as barriers to scaling digital agricultural platforms. These limitations directly reduce the trialability and observability of innovations, two key attributes necessary for adoption, according to DoI theory (Rogers, 2003).

The third constraint is institutional and governance weakness. In many emerging markets, digital circular technologies exist in a legal and regulatory vacuum. Blockchain-based approaches to e-waste tracking or carbon accounting often face prohibitive ambiguity because national governments lag in issuing enforceable digital and environmental standards. Tabe-Ojong et al. (2024) observed that many countries in North Africa and Central Asia have not progressed beyond pilot projects due to poor policy coordination and insufficient regulatory clarity for platform-based climate tools. Such "pilot-to-scale" gap reflects an institutional incapacity to support continuity, enforceability, and data stewardship.

A fourth and critical challenge stems from skill mismatches, specifically the lack of digital literacy and understanding of circular economy principles. Hernandez-Aguilera et al. (2020) argued that farmers often resist digital tools not because of cultural resistance but because of exclusion from platform governance, opacity in data ownership, and fear of being transformed into "data labourers". In Latin America, rural communities continue to face digital exclusion even as cities such as Curitiba and Medellín lead in urban circular innovation (GSMA, 2018). This rural–urban divide undermines the equitable scaling of circular technologies.

2.6 Strategies for Inclusive and Accelerated Adoption of Circular and Net-Zero Technologies

Achievement of widespread adoption of digital circular and climate technologies in emerging markets requires more than just access to innovation. It demands strategic governance frameworks, inclusive designs, institutional experimentation, and targeted financing. The prevailing diffusion challenges (ranging from infrastructure voids to governance gaps) underscore the need for coordinated policy and investment responses across multiple scales. This section outlines six strategic levers that support inclusive and accelerated technology adoption.

1. **National Digital Circular Economy Strategies**

Emerging economies must launch digital innovation within broader sustainability transitions via national strategies that explicitly link circular economy goals with climate policy. Some countries (e.g., Colombia, Brazil) have launched integrated circular economy roadmaps that prioritise digital innovation for resource efficiency, lifecycle monitoring, as well as waste reduction (Ecomondo, 2023). These frameworks serve to align ministries, private actors, and civil society under a common agenda, thereby improving coordination and investment signals.

2. **Regulatory Sandboxes and Policy Experimentation**

Regulatory sandboxes, defined as controlled environments for testing new technologies, serve as a crucial mechanism for reconciling innovation with legislative frameworks. Circular technologies, such as blockchain-based carbon credit systems and digital product passports, frequently face legislative uncertainty. Sandboxes facilitate the assessment of risks by regulators while enabling innovators to refine use cases with actual users. The UN Climate Technology Centre and Network (CTCN) has advocated for African governments to consider establishing sandbox platforms to test circular data protocols and emission-tracking technologies (CTCN, 2022). Although only a limited number of sandboxes are currently operational, there is growing policy momentum across major African economies.

3. **Green Public Procurement (GPP)**

Government procurement is a powerful mechanism to stimulate early demand for circular and net-zero technologies. By integrating sustainability criteria into tenders (e.g., lifecycle carbon footprint, recyclability, and data transparency), public institutions can mainstream otherwise niche technologies. Lee (2023) identified GPP as a critical enabler of circularity-led innovation diffusion, particularly in sectors such as e-waste recovery, smart buildings, as well as sustainable mobility.

4. **Public–Private Partnerships (PPPs) for Local Access**

Adoption requires contextual tailoring. Effective public–private partnerships in the telecom, agri-tech, and e-waste sectors offer a viable route to reach last-mile users while sharing risks and costs. In India and Kenya, telecom–agriculture PPPs have connected smallholder farmers to climate advisory services via mobile platforms (Hernandez-Aguilera et al., 2020; Suresh et al., 2025). In Latin America, municipal–private initiatives have scaled blockchain-based traceability tools for circular city initiatives (Ecomondo, 2023).

5. **Development Finance for Circular Digital Infrastructure**

Multilateral and development finance institutions must prioritise circular digital infrastructure (e.g., cloud storage, fibre-optic networks, sensor networks) through targeted grants, blended finance, as well as results-based instruments. The CTCN (2022) reported that most African nations lack dedicated funding channels to support the digital infrastructure required for a circular transition. Institutions such as the African Development Bank and the Inter-American Development Bank (IDB) have begun issuing green bonds with earmarked funds for digital resource-efficiency tools, yet significant gaps remain.

6. **Regional Platforms for Technology Transfer and Knowledge Sharing**

Initiatives such as the African Circular Economy Alliance and the Latin American Circular Economy Coalition serve as regional platforms to facilitate peer learning, develop regional standards, and provide open-source digital toolkits (CTCN, 2022; Ecomondo, 2023). These platforms promote South–South collaboration, avoiding dependence on proprietary systems and external technologies that are misaligned with local contexts.

2.7 Conclusion

Digital technologies possess the transformative potential to accelerate net-zero and circular transitions in the Global South. However, realisation of this promise depends on three interlinked factors: contextual compatibility, institutional readiness, and the strength of inclusive innovation ecosystems. In this chapter, we demonstrated that while technologies such as AI, IoT, and digital twins offer high observability and applicability in urban and semi-urban settings, others (e.g., blockchain, quantum computing) require stronger regulatory scaffolding and investment alignment. We showed that technical sophistication alone cannot ensure adoption. Instead, institutional design, adaptive governance, and capacity-building remain decisive. We also highlighted that diffusion challenges (e.g., infrastructure gaps, regulatory ambiguity, and digital illiteracy) continue to constrain scale.

Policymakers must prioritise context-matching: aligning technologies with local climate and circular priorities, investing in platforms and people, as well as coordinating across public, private, and multilateral actors. The DoI and institutional theory frameworks offer robust tools for crafting adaptive, equity-oriented interventions. Ultimately, a smart circular transition depends not only on digital capacity but also on policy imagination and institutional agility in the face of accelerating climate risks.

Future research should investigate (1) effective institutional mechanisms for scaling digital circular solutions in informal and peri-urban contexts; (2) metrics and evaluation tools to assess observability and trialability across use cases; and (3) comparative analyses of regulatory sandboxes and their efficacy in catalysing trust in carbon and circular data systems.

References

Adamidis, C., Craven, A., Dober, D., & Alexandris, G. (n.d.). *A framework for pairing circular economy and IoT*. Maastricht University Press. https://pubpub.maastrichtuniversitypress.nl/pub/p7va5i8z/release/1

Advanced Info Service (AIS). (n.d.). *AIS redesigns the E-Waste ecosystem with Blockchain on E-Waste for the first time in the Southeast Asia region: TGO and six green network partners have joined forces to power a sustainable environment*. AIS Sustainability. https://sustainability.ais.co.th/en/update/news/279/ais-redesigns-the-e-waste-ecosystem-with-blockchain-on-e-waste-for-the-first-time-in-the-southeast-asia-region-tgo-and-six-green-network-partners-have-joined-forces-to-power-a-sustainable-env

Ali, Z. A., Zain, M., Hasan, R., Pathan, M. S., AlSalman, H., & Almisned, F. A. (2025). Digital twins: Cornerstone to circular economy and sustainability goals. *Environment, Development and Sustainability*. https://doi.org/10.1007/s10668-025-06221-4

Amankwah-Amoah, J., & Hinson, R. E. (2024). Scaling up and scaling out of darkness: Elucidating the influences of institutional dysfunction in scaling up solar PV in sub-Saharan Africa. *World Development*, *183*, 106726.

Awasthi, A. K., Zeng, X., & Li, J. (2016). Environmental pollution of electronic waste recycling in India: A critical review. *Environmental Pollution, 211*, 259–270.

Balci, G., & Ali, S. I. (2024). The relationship between information processing capabilities, net-zero capability, and supply chain performance. *Supply Chain Management, 29*(2), 351–370. https://doi.org/10.1108/scm-06-2023-0320

Brahim, M., & Lahiani, A. (2025). Smart waste management. In *Global pathways for efficient waste management and inclusive economic development* (pp. 53–96). Springer. https://doi.org/10.1007/978-981-96-5569-4_4

Business Tech Africa. (2025, May 15). *Optimising supply chains with AI: Addressing Africa's challenges*. https://www.businesstechafrica.co.za/business/trade-and-commerce/2025/05/15/optimising-supply-chains-with-ai-addressing-africas-challenges/

Chapungu, L., Togo, M., & Raimundo, I. (2024). Prospects and challenges for adopting artificial intelligence and digital tools in climate resilience in rural Southern Africa: A systematic review. In *Climate change resilience in Rural Southern Africa* (pp. 215–229). Springer. https://doi.org/10.1007/978-3-031-73600-1_15

Choruma, D. J., Dirwai, T. L., Mutenje, M. J., Mustafa, M., Chimonyo, V. G. P., Jacobs-Mata, I., & Mabhaudhi, T. (2024). Digitalisation in agriculture: A scoping review of technologies in practice, challenges, and opportunities for smallholder farmers in sub-saharan africa. *Journal of agriculture and food research*, *18*, 101286.

Climate Technology Centre and Network (CTCN). (2022). *Circular economy and climate technology solutions for Africa*. United Nations Environment Programme. https://www.ctc-n.org/sites/default/files/CTCN_Circular_Economy_Africa_Fin.pdf

Ecomondo. (2023). *Circular economy in Latin America and the Caribbean: A shared vision*. https://www.ecomondo.com/Data/Ecomondo/Ricerche%20e%20Rapporti/Inglese/-english-circular-economy-in-latin-america-and-the-caribbean_-a-shared-vision.pdf

Elbashir, M., & Desikachari, K. B. (2025). *India's path to AI autonomy: A three-pillar strategy*. Atlantic Council. https://www.atlanticcouncil.org/in-depth-research-reports/issue-brief/indias-path-to-ai-autonomy/

Godefroit-Winkel, D. (2023). An institutional perspective on climate change, markets, and consumption across three countries. *Markets, Globalization & Development Review, 7*(4). https://digitalcommons.uri.edu/mgdr/vol7/iss4/4/

GSMA. (2018). *Technology for climate action in Latin America and the Caribbean*. https://www.gsma.com/about-us/regions/latin-america/wp-content/uploads/2018/06/Technology-for-Climate-Action-in-Latin-America-and-the-Caribbean.pdf

GSMA. (2021). *Digital agriculture maps: 2021 state of the sector in low and middle-income countries*. https://www.gsma.com/mobilefordevelopment/resources/digital-agriculture-maps-2021

Hariyani, D., Hariyani, P., Mishra, S., & Sharma, M. K. (2024). Leveraging digital technologies for advancing circular economy practices and enhancing life cycle analysis: A systematic literature review. *Waste Management & Research Bulletin*, 6, 007. https://doi.org/10.1016/j.wmb.2024.06.007

Hernandez-Aguilera, J. N., Loboguerrero Rodriguez, A. M., Herrera, A., & Baethgen, W. (2020, August 5). *Harnessing digital tools for climate and agriculture*. CGIAR/CCAFS. https://ccafs.cgiar.org/news/harnessing-digital-tools-climate-and-agriculture

Izuchukwu P., O., Zino Izu, O., F. Chudi, & T. Ojevwe, A. (2025). Public-private collaborations in waste management evaluating policy effectiveness and governance models in Nigeria. *Journal of Integrity Ecosystems and Environment*, *3*(2), 25–53.

Lee, S. Y. (2023). Net-zero transitions for all? Considering applications in Asia. *Sustainability Science*, *18*(5), 2053–2058. https://doi.org/10.1007/s11625-023-01409-x

Li, Y., Antwi-Afari, M. F., Anwer, S., Mehmood, I., Umer, W., Mohandes, S. R., Wuni, I. Y., Abdul-Rahman, M., & Li, H. (2024). Artificial intelligence in net-zero carbon emissions for sustainable building projects: A systematic literature and science mapping review. *Buildings, 14*(9), 2752. https://doi.org/10.3390/buildings14092752

Maksimovic, M. (2017). The role of green Internet of Things (G-IoT) and big data in making cities smarter, safer and more sustainable. *International Journal of Computing and Digital Systems, 6*(4), 2210–142. https://doi.org/10.12785/ijcds/060403

Matewos, T. (2019). Deconstructing institutional roles in climate change adaptation: The case of local public institutions in drought-prone districts of Sidama, Southern Ethiopia. *Environmental Science & Policy, 99*, 14–22. https://doi.org/10.1016/j.envsci.2019.05.005

Meng, X., Das, S., & Meng, J. (2023). Integration of digital twin and circular economy in the construction industry. *Sustainability, 15*(17), 13186. https://doi.org/10.3390/su151713186

Mondal, S., Das, S., & Vrana, V. G. (2024). Exploring the role of artificial intelligence in achieving a net-zero carbon economy in emerging economies. *Sustainability, 16*(23), 10299. https://doi.org/10.3390/su162310299

Olawade, D. B., Wada, O. Z., David-Olawade, A. C., Fapohunda, O., Ige, A. O., & Ling, J. (2024). Artificial intelligence potential for net-zero sustainability: Current evidence and prospects. *NPJ Nexus Sustainability, 1*(1), 100041. https://doi.org/10.1016/j.nxsust.2024.100041

Pakseresht, A., Yavari, A., Kaliji, S. A., & Hakelius, K. (2022). The intersection of blockchain technology and circular economy in the agri-food sector. *Sustainable Production and Consumption, 32*, 731–742. https://doi.org/10.1016/j.spc.2022.11.002

Rejeb, A., Suhaiza, Z., Rejeb, K., Seuring, S., & Treiblmaier, H. (2022). The Internet of Things and the circular economy: A systematic literature review and research agenda. *Journal of Cleaner Production, 367*, 131439. https://doi.org/10.1016/j.jclepro.2022.131439

Rogers, E. M. (2003). *Diffusion of innovations* (5th ed.). Free Press.

Scott, W. R. (2008). *Institutions and organizations: Ideas and interests* (3rd ed.). Sage.

Suresh, D., Shaw, R., & Masutomi, Y. (2025). Farmers' perspective on digitalization of climate-smart agricultural practices: A comparative study in Tamil Nadu, India. *Discover Agriculture, 3*, Article 28. https://doi.org/10.1007/s44279-025-00176-w

SYSTEMIQ. (2023). *AI and the climate transition: Aligning capital, code and carbon*. Grantham Research Institute. https://www.systemiq.earth/ai-and-the-climate-transition-aligning-capital-code-and-carbon/

Tabe-Ojong, M. P., Jr., Salama, Y., Abay, K. A., Abdelaziz, F., Zaccari, C., Akramkhanov, A., Menza, G., & Anarbekov, O. (2024). Harnessing digital innovations for climate action and market access: Opportunities and constraints in the CWANA region. *Global Food Security, 38*, 100763. https://doi.org/10.1016/j.gfs.2024.100763

Tan, A. (2024, November 18). *Strategies for sustainable engineering in Asia beyond 2025*. FutureIoT. https://futureiot.tech/strategies-for-sustainable-engineering-in-asia-beyond-2025/

Tang, A., Tchao, E. T., Agbemenu, A. S., Keelson, E., Klogo, G. S., & Kponyo, J. J. (2024). Assessing blockchain and IoT technologies for agricultural food supply chains in Africa: A feasibility analysis. *Heliyon*, *10*(15).

TheCryptoQueen. (2018, August 15). *Blockchain taskforce to enable food tracking using blockchain technology, says Bitange Ndemo*. BitKE. https://bitcoinke.io/2018/08/blockchain-taskforce-to-enable-blockchain-food-tracking/

World Bank. (2024, March 4). *Digital progress and trends report: Interactive charts—Digital adoption*. https://www.worldbank.org/en/data/interactive/2024/03/04/digital-progress-and-trends-report-interactive-charts

World Development Indicators (2025). *World Bank DataBank*. Retrieved May 13, 2025, from https://databank.worldbank.org/reports.aspx?source=world-development-indicators

PART II

Pathways to Implementation

CHAPTER 3

Corporate Pathways to Net-Zero and Circular Economy Transition

Abstract This chapter examines how emerging-market firms pursue net-zero and circular economy goals amid institutional fragility, limited financing, and capability gaps. Drawing on the resource-based view, it analyses how technological, financial and human resources influence the credibility and execution of climate commitments. Sustainability integration is explored through practices such as emissions tracking, product redesign, and reverse logistics, while considering contextual challenges, including fragmented supply chains and informal economies. The chapter highlights the enabling roles of blended finance, innovation ecosystems, and adaptive policy frameworks. While some firms demonstrate progress, the majority remain in symbolic compliance. Strategic enablers and context-specific solutions are outlined, with an emphasis on capability development and institutional alignment.

Keywords Net-zero transition · Circular economy · Emerging markets · Green entrepreneurship · Sustainability integration · Blended finance · Institutional alignment

O. Evans and O. Adeola, *Innovations in Circular Economy and Net Zero*, https://doi.org/10.1007/978-3-032-22094-3_3

3.1 Introduction

In the context of emerging markets, corporate sustainability is increasingly positioned at the intersection of two critical global objectives: the urgent shift towards net-zero emissions and the integration of circular economy principles. As scrutiny from governments, investors, and civil society actors intensifies regarding climate-related issues, companies are under escalating pressure to devise strategies that not only mitigate environmental impact but also sustain their long-term competitiveness. These transitions in emerging markets occur within a structurally intricate environment characterised by institutional fragility, uneven financial access, and a limited capacity to absorb new technologies (Asia Investor Group on Climate Change [AIGCC], 2024; Climate Investment Funds, 2025). Such constraints necessitate a customised approach to corporate climate strategy, one that accounts for regional disparities and firm-specific differences in governance structures, resource availability, and sectoral vulnerabilities.

In this chapter, we examine how firms in emerging markets engage in net-zero and circular economy transitions, with respect to both public disclosure and implementation practices. We evaluate the credibility of corporate sustainability pledges, interrogate strategic and institutional constraints that impede effective implementation, and propose pathways for capability development and policy reform. Specifically, we analyse corporate decarbonisation efforts, the financial and regulatory structures that support or constrain them, as well as the extent to which firms internalise circularity via innovation, reverse logistics, and product redesign. We also assess the role of informal actors, supply chain fragmentation, and blended finance in corporate outcomes. To guide this analysis, we apply the resource-based view (RBV) as a conceptual lens. RBV posits that firms gain sustained advantage when they leverage internal resources (e.g., technological, human, financial) that are valuable, rare, inimitable, and organisationally embedded (Barney, 1991). This lens is particularly relevant in the resource-constrained environments of emerging markets, where external institutional support is uneven.

3.2 Greenpreneurs in Emerging Markets

Emerging markets are increasingly recognised as critical arenas for catalysing climate action through entrepreneurship. The Global Green Growth Institute (GGGI) has strategically leveraged this potential through its *Greenpreneurs* initiative, which promotes green entrepreneurship by targeting youth- and women-led climate-tech startups across developing countries. Between 2018 and 2023, the program supported more than 556 startups across various growth stages (ideation, pre-seed, and seed), providing mentoring, technical assistance, seed funding, and investor matchmaking (GGGI, 2024). This multi-pronged approach illustrates how entrepreneurship can bridge gaps in green growth, employment, and sustainability, particularly in contexts where institutional voids and financing constraints hinder climate innovation. A parallel insight from the *Southeast Asia Green Economy Report* reinforces this dynamic. While over 90% of climate investors are ready to invest in the region, only 25% of firms are deemed investment-ready, highlighting systemic gaps in capacity and business model maturity (Bain & Company et al., 2024).

A key finding from the Greenpreneurs initiative is the regional variance in startup outcomes, which reveals both systemic weaknesses and pockets of excellence. For instance, the Pacific Islands emerged as a standout region, with over 230 businesses supported and more than 700 green jobs created (300+ of which are held by women) (GGGI, 2024). In contrast, despite Southeast Asia's robust industrial base and growing climate capital inflows, its participation in Greenpreneurs' programs has been comparatively low. This paradox is echoed in the Bain & Company et al. (2024) report, which classifies 60–70% of Southeast Asian firms as "transitioners" (those experimenting with green initiatives but lacking formal targets or viable decarbonisation strategies). GGGI's forthcoming accelerator in Vietnam represents a strategic pivot to enhance green entrepreneurial readiness in regions that require scalable climate-tech solutions, particularly in energy efficiency, manufacturing, and supply chains.

The intersection of gender, entrepreneurship, and climate action is a prominent feature of the GGGI program's outcomes. Across all Greenpreneurs cohorts, 201 businesses were identified as having at least one female founder, affirming the growing role of women in the green economy (GGGI, 2024). This aligns with broader research highlighting the transformative impact of women-led enterprises on sustainable development (Abril, 2024; Ahmed, 2025). Moreover, firms in Southeast Asia's green economy are increasingly engaging with women at the grassroots level (e.g., agriculture, carbon projects, circular logistics) (Bain & Company et al., 2024). For example, in the Philippines, GGGI-supported agri-cooperatives involving female farmers have generated significant employment and contributed to community resilience (GGGI, 2024), illustrating the multiplier effect of gender-inclusive entrepreneurship on local green transitions.

The Greenpreneurs model has also shown the potential to unlock post-incubation capital, although access remains uneven. Colombia's mature startups, particularly under the MAPBiO and PPTAF programs, collectively raised over $27 million, representing nearly 72% of capital mobilised through Greenpreneurs globally (GGGI, 2024). These successes stem from supportive ecosystems, strong public–private linkages, and proven commercialisation paths. By contrast, Southeast Asian SMEs face structural barriers similar to those observed in smaller Greenpreneurs markets, such as Kiribati or Saint Lucia. Bain & Company et al. (2024) report that only 1 in 4 Southeast Asian SMEs has an actionable sustainability plan, despite mounting pressure from multinational corporations to decarbonise supply chains and disclose Scope 3 emissions. These insights support Nugraha et al.'s (2006) argument that thriving entrepreneurial ecosystems require not just talent but also coherent policy frameworks and enabling financial infrastructure.

Equally instructive is the importance of cultural and institutional alignment in shaping firm-level outcomes. Sahertian et al. (2016) highlight the case of Indonesia's batik industry, where local wisdom and ethical entrepreneurship transformed traditional SMEs into environmentally responsible enterprises. GGGI's Greenpreneurs programe echoes this philosophy by localising training and business models across its interventions, from eco-fashion in Uganda and carbon farming in Fiji to bioeconomy ventures in Colombia. These culturally grounded approaches align with findings from the Southeast Asia report, which notes that some firms (e.g., Sembcorp Industries in Singapore, ACEN in the Philippines) have successfully integrated corporate strategies with decarbonisation goals (Bain & Company et al., 2024). Local adaptation, when combined with technical innovation and supportive policy frameworks, emerges as a key enabler of sustained green transformation in both SMEs and large corporates.

Thus, the success of the Greenpreneurs initiative in emerging markets illustrates how entrepreneurship can serve as a transformative pathway towards net-zero and circular economies. However, scaling this model requires overcoming persistent barriers (e.g., financing bottlenecks, regulatory uncertainty, and limited access to strategic partnerships). The Southeast Asia Green Economy Report (Bain & Company et al., 2024) highlights a significant opportunity among "transitioner" firms that lack net-zero roadmaps but are open to change, a demographic that closely aligns with the Greenpreneurs' target audience. Strategic collaboration with corporate actors, venture funds, and development banks is essential to expand these initiatives. As Hlahla et al. (2016) assert, green economy efforts are most effective when grassroots innovation is supported by institutional and financial scaffolding. Integrating greenpreneurship into national policy frameworks, while mobilising corporate climate leadership, will be central to unlocking inclusive green growth across the Global South.

3.3 The Credibility of Net-Zero Commitments in Emerging Markets

In recent years, corporate commitments to achieving net-zero emissions in emerging markets have increased significantly; however, concerns persist regarding their credibility and practical enforceability. Although numerous firms in Sub-Saharan Africa, Southeast Asia, and Latin America have declared intentions to achieve net-zero emissions by mid-century, most have not supported these pledges with comprehensive transition plans, capital investment frameworks, or sectoral roadmaps. For example, PwC (2023) reported that while over 70% of large listed companies in Asia-Pacific markets now publish sustainability statements, fewer than 25% provide science-based emissions reduction targets aligned with the Paris Agreement. Similarly, the Africa Finance Corporation (2023) observed that although African firms increasingly express low-carbon aspirations, fewer than 15% of these statements result in enforceable decarbonisation strategies. In Latin America, the Axon Partners Group (2023) identified a comparable trend: more than 80% of climate disclosures in Brazil and Mexico lack third-party validation or sector-specific benchmarks. This disconnect between ambition and actionable commitment remains a defining characteristic of the climate-credibility gap.

Greenwashing concerns have further undermined the credibility of net-zero pledges in emerging markets. A comprehensive review by Kahlen et al. (2021) found that, globally, corporate net-zero targets would reduce baseline emissions by only about 40% on average, with many firms employing offset-heavy accounting or setting overly deferred targets. In emerging economies, where regulatory oversight and market discipline remain weak, firms often leverage voluntary disclosures to project climate ambitions while failing to implement credible decarbonisation. Chan et al. (2024) emphasise the importance of distinguishing "transition ambition" (the stated target) from "transition capacity", which encompasses the financial, technological, and managerial resources required to achieve decarbonisation. Without robust verification mechanisms, transition declarations risk functioning as reputational shields, rather than reliable indicators of genuine corporate transformation.

Discrepancies in reporting practices further exacerbate credibility challenges. The Asian Development Bank (2023) documented that although sustainability reporting has expanded across Southeast Asia, data quality and comparability remain poor due to fragmented taxonomies and the absence of standardised metrics. A similar pattern is evident in Latin America, where national regulations rarely mandate the disclosure of material climate risks or scope 3 emissions. Many firms report only partial emissions inventories or omit high-impact supply chain emissions. Additionally, inconsistent reporting timelines complicate year-on-year comparisons. These inconsistencies undermine investor confidence and hinder regulators' ability to monitor progress or enforce compliance.

The absence of third-party verification significantly undermines the legitimacy of many net-zero claims. In emerging markets, independent assurance of sustainability reports remains an exception rather than the norm. According to the Task Force on Climate-related Financial Disclosures (2023), less than one-third of the firms in low- and middle-income countries submit climate disclosures to external auditors or verification bodies. This lack of validation creates opportunities for data manipulation and diminishes the credibility of self-reported emissions data. Additionally, the Science Based Targets initiative (SBTi, 2024) observed that only 4% of validated corporate science-based targets originated from Africa and Latin America combined, with just 1.2% from Africa and 2.8% from Latin America. This low level of regional integration into global accountability platforms highlights persistent structural gaps in climate governance and corporate transparency.

Emerging markets face specific institutional and economic constraints that hinder the adoption of rigorous disclosure frameworks, such as the Task Force on Climate-Related Financial Disclosures (TCFD) or the Science-Based Targets Initiative (SBTi). While the TCFD framework has gained traction in Europe and North America, its implementation is uneven in the Global South. Regulatory authorities in many African and Southeast Asian countries often lack the capacity or political mandates to enforce detailed disclosure obligations. Moreover, firms in these regions frequently cite the high cost of compliance, limited expertise in emissions accounting, and inadequate data infrastructure as key barriers to adoption (ADB, 2023; AFC, 2023). Although voluntary uptake is increasing, most participating firms are multinational subsidiaries or publicly listed conglomerates. Small- and medium-sized enterprises (SMEs), which account for over 80% of employment in many emerging economies (ADB, 2023), are largely excluded. This exclusion represents a form of systemic risk to inclusive climate transitions.

Some firms have nonetheless begun to demonstrate credible transition planning through the adoption of sector-specific benchmarks and early-stage emissions reduction. The SBTi (2024) reported that companies in high-emission sectors (e.g., energy and cement in Brazil and India) have initiated decarbonisation efforts through process redesign, energy efficiency improvements, and the substitution of feedstock inputs. Although such examples remain limited, they illustrate the potential for credible action when policy incentives, investor pressure, and access to international financing converge. These cases underscore the importance of integrating context-specific standards and support mechanisms tailored to emerging economies, rather than importing rigid frameworks from developed markets.

3.4 Environmental Governance Performance as a Competitive Advantage

Environmental governance performance is increasingly emerging as a strategic differentiator for firms in emerging markets. Companies that rigorously integrate Environmental, Social, and Governance (ESG) principles into their core operations gain quantifiable advantages in access to capital, expansion of market presence, attraction of consumers, and fostering of innovation (Cahyono et al., 2024; Prodanova & Tarasova, 2024). Evidence from Latin America, Asia, and Africa demonstrates that environmental governance excellence not only aligns with global compliance trends but also yields tangible commercial returns. Emerging market leaders such as Arçelik, Natura, Infosys, Geely, and Siam Cement demonstrate that sustainability-oriented strategies improve market access, lower capital costs, promote consumer engagement, and enable disruptive innovation (Tansan et al., 2023). Their experiences validate the claim that environmental governance integration (when rigorous, verifiable, and embedded in corporate strategy) serves not as a constraint but as a durable advantage.

One of the most immediate benefits of environmental governance leadership is enhanced market access (Cahyono et al., 2024). Developed markets have introduced regulations requiring exporters to demonstrate sustainability across their supply chains. For example, the European Union's Carbon Border Adjustment Mechanism mandates emissions reporting for imports and will impose tariffs based on carbon intensity. In response, emerging market firms with verifiable ESG records enjoy a first-mover advantage. Arçelik, a leading Turkish appliance manufacturer, proactively reduced emissions across its operations and supply chain, while employing accredited auditors to monitor supplier compliance (Tansan et al., 2023). These actions enabled the firm to maintain and expand its market share within the EU (its largest export destination) despite tightening environmental standards.

Sustainability performance also enhances a company's access to investment capital and reduces financing costs (Cahyono et al., 2024). ESG-focused assets under management in emerging markets increased by approximately 80% between 2018 and 2021, indicating growing investor confidence in firms with high environmental governance ratings (Tansan et al., 2023). The MSCI Emerging Markets ESG Leaders Index outperformed its broader market counterpart by 54% in 2021, suggesting a correlation between ESG scores and market returns. However, this relationship does not imply direct causation and remains sensitive to sectoral and macroeconomic variables.

Green bonds and sustainability-linked loans exemplify how ESG commitments are reshaping financial instruments. Green bonds, which finance environmental projects, attract ESG-mandated funds and often secure more favourable terms than traditional debt. Arçelik issued a €350 million green bond with a 3% coupon, which was five times oversubscribed. Similarly, Geely Automobile, a Chinese carmaker, issued a $400 million overseas green bond, marking a first for China's automotive sector

(Tansan et al., 2023). In Latin America, Brazil and Chile have emerged as pioneers in sovereign green bond issuance, funding initiatives in renewable energy and sustainable agriculture (Singh, 2025). These issuances signal a growing appetite for climate-aligned financial instruments across the region.

Empirical evidence indicates that leadership in environmental governance positively influences brand equity and consumer preferences. A survey conducted by BCG reveals that a significant number of consumers in emerging markets consider sustainability when purchasing snacks. Although willingness to pay a premium remains limited, consumers in these markets express concerns about the environmental and social impacts across sectors such as travel, apparel, and energy (Tansan et al., 2023). Natura, Brazil's leading cosmetics brand, has effectively capitalised on these consumer preferences by sourcing Amazonian ingredients through sustainable practices and by launching the Ekos line, which aligns directly with consumer values concerning biodiversity protection (Tansan et al., 2023). Furthermore, an orientation towards environmental governance enhances a firm's capacity to attract and retain talent. Approximately 70% of Generation Z workers prefer employers with demonstrable commitments to environmental governance (Tansan et al., 2023). Infosys, an Indian IT services firm, leveraged its achievement of the carbon neutrality milestone in 2020 and its proactive diversity policies to enhance its employer brand equity (Tansan et al., 2023), thereby supporting its inclusion in global top employer rankings.

Beyond risk mitigation and reputation gains, environmental governance performance also unlocks innovation. Siam Cement's "Zero Burn" project in Thailand exemplifies how sustainable practices can drive the development of new business models. By converting agricultural waste into industrial fuel, the company reduced its carbon footprint while supporting local communities (Tansan et al., 2023). In Africa, South Africa's 2019 Carbon Tax Act catalysed alignment of environmental governance across industries, with the Johannesburg Stock Exchange reinforcing disclosure standards through its Socially Responsible Index (Tygart, 2025). These institutional shifts incentivised firms to innovate in cleaner production and reporting practices.

Despite notable successes in environmental governance among leading firms, significant structural disparities persist across emerging markets. Small and medium-sized enterprises (SMEs) in the Middle East and

North Africa exhibit particularly weak environmental governance performance, especially in environmental stewardship, even after controlling for income levels (Ferrazzi & Tueske, 2023). A broader analysis supports this trend: companies in ten key emerging markets (e.g., Argentina, Brazil, India, and Turkey) average an environmental sustainability score of just 48, compared to 64 among their G20 counterparts (Tansan et al., 2023). Figure 3.1 summarises the performance gap between emerging- and developed-market companies across ESG metrics. Several factors contribute to this gap. Developed markets began adopting ESG frameworks decades earlier, catalysed by regulatory pressure and civil society advocacy. In contrast, many emerging economies have prioritised economic growth over environmental and social governance, which results in less mature policy environments and weaker disclosure norms. In emissions-intensive industries (e.g., steel and transport), firms also face technical and financial barriers to decarbonisation. Moreover, many companies (particularly unlisted ones) lack ESG reporting experience and often divert resources towards urgent local development needs, such as job creation and poverty alleviation (Tansan et al., 2023). These systemic challenges underscore the need for tailored policy frameworks, capacity-building initiatives, as well as localised ESG assessment models that reflect regional development contexts while enabling firms to close performance gaps.

3.5 Corporate Capabilities and Constraints: A Resource-Based View

The RBV offers a strategic framework for assessing corporate readiness to undertake climate transitions. RBV posits that firms gain competitive advantage through the deployment of resources that are valuable, rare, inimitable, and organisationally embedded (Barney, 1991). In terms of decarbonisation, these resources include technological innovation, financial capital, skilled human resources, and institutional routines that align climate goals with operational capacity. For firms in emerging markets, resource asymmetries, rather than ambition gaps, often determine the credibility and effectiveness of net-zero commitments.

Technological capability is a decisive factor in the implementation of climate strategies. Firms that possess proprietary tools for emissions measurement and energy optimisation gain a competitive edge in aligning with science-based targets. In 2024, Asuene Inc. partnered with

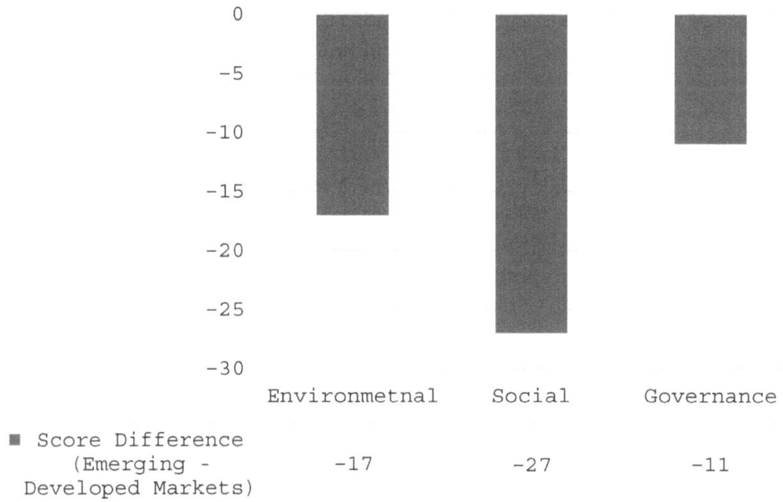

Fig. 3.1 Difference between the average emerging market company score and the average developed market company score (*Data source* Tansan et al. [2023]. *Note* Negative values indicate that emerging market companies score lower than developed market companies across all ESG pillars)

Artemeter LLC to expand AI-enabled carbon accounting solutions across the Asia-Pacific region, enabling companies to conduct granular emissions tracking and real-time benchmarking (Asuene, 2024). In contrast, many companies in Latin America and Africa still rely on manual tracking systems, which limit both precision and speed of reporting. This digital infrastructure gap constrains firms' ability to respond swiftly to evolving regulatory and investor expectations (Clean Air Fund, 2022).

Financial capacity also plays a critical role in shaping a firm's decarbonisation trajectory. Firms with access to patient capital and climate-aligned financial instruments are better positioned to adopt long-term, low-carbon solutions without immediate pressure to deliver returns. According to the Climate Investment Funds (CIF) (2025), firms in countries such as South Africa, India, and Indonesia are piloting large-scale industrial decarbonisation supported by concessional funding and blended finance mechanisms linked to their national eligibility under the CIF's Industry Transition program. In contrast, firms in smaller economies face high capital costs, limited access to ESG-linked loan structures, and underdeveloped green bond markets. These financing constraints disproportionately affect local firms and small to mid-sized enterprises, which often struggle to participate in global climate investment flows.

Human resource capability plays a critical role in determining whether firms can internalise sustainability knowledge and align climate strategies with core operations. Companies with trained personnel in emissions accounting, energy modelling, and climate risk evaluation build internal credibility and execution strength. However, across emerging markets, these competencies are unevenly distributed. The Clean Air Fund (2022) reported that many cities in Africa and Latin America lack skilled technical teams to support data-driven climate planning, which reflects broader labour market shortages in private firms in these regions. Capacity-building must therefore extend beyond disclosure mandates to include sustained investment in workforce development and environmental education within firms.

Organisational systems and routines further differentiate firms that successfully translate sustainability commitments into action. The AIGCC (2024) reported that fewer than one-quarter of high-emitting companies in Asia and Latin America have fully articulated transition plans with interim targets, board oversight, alongside capital expenditure alignment. Even fewer companies link net-zero goals to executive compensation or product redesign. This lack of organisational integration reflects capability constraints, not only in resources but also in strategic cohesion. RBV emphasises that resources must be embedded in firm structures and decision-making processes to generate sustained competitive advantage (Barney, 1991). Without such embeddedness, sustainability remains peripheral rather than transformative.

Some firms have nonetheless demonstrated resource-led leadership. In Latin America, SLR Consulting (2025) has advised firms in manufacturing and extractives on decarbonisation strategies tailored to resource availability and sectoral emissions profiles. Supported by international partners, these firms have developed closed-loop production processes, conducted full lifecycle assessments, and initiated the greening of their procurement systems. Such cases illustrate how external advisory services can complement internal capabilities, particularly where firms lack in-house expertise but possess strategic intent.

However, significant capability gaps persist across emerging market firms. AIGCC (2024) concluded that most corporate decarbonisation plans in Asia and Africa fall short of credible transition thresholds due to inadequate resource mobilisation. These gaps include not only tangible resources (e.g., funding, technology) but also intangible elements (e.g., climate leadership, learning orientation, employee empowerment). The RBV emphasises that even where external financing or regulation exists, firms that fail to cultivate internal capabilities will struggle to sustain competitive adaptation in the low-carbon economy.

3.6 Barriers to Corporate Transition: Institutions, Finance, and Expertise

Firms in emerging markets face a constellation of barriers that undermine credible decarbonisation. Chief among these is weak regulatory enforcement. While many governments have adopted national climate plans, implementation is often fragile or politically constrained. AIGCC (2024) found that among the top 100 emitting companies in emerging Asia, only 24% faced consistent regulatory monitoring of climate disclosures. In many countries, institutional weakness manifests as overlapping agency mandates, insufficient coordination between ministries, and the absence of carbon pricing regimes, all of which contribute to inconsistent enforcement (Zhou et al., 2025). Without institutional strength, regulatory frameworks often lack the necessary pressure and guidance to move firms from intention to execution.

Financial constraints further erode the credibility of transition efforts in emerging markets. Limited access to long-term capital, underdeveloped green finance ecosystems, and high perceived investment risk discourage firms from investing in energy-efficient infrastructure or process redesigns. The Climate Investment Funds (2025) prioritised seven countries for industrial decarbonisation; firms outside these pilot states have had limited access to concessional funding and advisory support. Available data also indicate that green bond issuance is concentrated among a few regional actors, particularly in South Africa, Chile, and India. Most local firms, especially small- and medium-sized enterprises, struggle to meet the due diligence and certification requirements necessary for sustainable finance, creating a two-tiered system of access. Furthermore, a study across 22 emerging markets found that credit-constrained firms were 30 percentage points less likely to plan green investments (De Haas et al., 2023), underscoring the systemic impact of capital inaccessibility.

Technical and managerial capacity constraints also hinder meaningful climate action. Across Africa, Latin America, and parts of Southeast Asia, firms face chronic shortages of personnel trained in emissions accounting, lifecycle analysis, or climate risk modelling. The Clean Air Fund (2022) reported that 12 city governments in these regions lacked skilled staff to manage urban decarbonisation initiatives, a trend mirrored in the corporate sector, where demand for ESG skills exceeds supply. Many firms rely on external consultants for compliance-oriented reporting; however, this approach does not build internal institutional knowledge or strategic ownership. Consequently, decarbonisation becomes a function of outsourcing, rather than in-house competence.

The institutional fragmentation of emerging economies intensifies barriers to effective climate action. Many countries operate dual economic systems: formal export-facing firms operate under global climate scrutiny, while informal sector actors, often unregistered or loosely regulated, dominate domestic value chains. This dynamic is particularly pronounced in the manufacturing and agriculture sectors. Informal firms account for the majority of employment in many African and South Asian economies; yet, their contributions to emissions remain largely undocumented (Clean Air Fund, 2022). Their exclusion limits the reach of climate policies and distorts data quality, creating blind spots in national decarbonisation pathways.

Supply chain fragmentation further hampers corporate decarbonisation. Multinational firms in emerging markets often rely on the patchwork of local suppliers, many of whom lack the systems or incentives to monitor and reduce their emissions. SLR Consulting (2025) observed that while some large manufacturers in Latin America had adopted decarbonisation strategies, they struggled to enforce ESG standards beyond Tier 1 suppliers. This breakdown in traceability affects scope 3 emissions, the most difficult and least reported component of corporate carbon footprints. The uneven uptake of global standards, such as the TCFD and International Sustainability Standards Board (ISSB), further complicates supplier engagement, as many local firms lack familiarity with or access to these disclosure tools (ISSB, 2024; TCFD, 2023). Without coordinated supply chain involvement, even well-intentioned net-zero strategies risk falling short of their target.

In contrast, firms in advanced economies benefit from policy stability, fiscal support, and technical ecosystems that reinforce corporate transition efforts. The Climate Investment Funds (2025) highlighted that early-stage decarbonisation initiatives in Europe and East Asia leveraged institutional support from national development banks and dedicated innovation clusters. These structures provide technical advisory, risk-sharing facilities, and regulatory certainty, none of which is consistently available in many developing countries. The absence of such enablers in emerging markets increases transition costs, delays capital allocation, and disincentivises corporate leadership.

3.7 Net-Zero and the Cost of Capital: Regional Disparities

The cost of capital is increasingly influenced not only by traditional financial metrics but also by climate-related risks and the credibility of a firm's decarbonisation strategy. In developed markets, firms that establish science-based net-zero targets and provide transparent emissions reports benefit from reduced borrowing costs and preferential access to capital (Paliampelou, 2024). This emerging green premium reflects investors' efforts to align portfolios with climate goals and hedge against regulatory or stranded-asset risks. However, this climate finance mechanism is weak or distorted in many emerging and developing economies (EDEs), where structural, institutional, and financial barriers prevent firms from fully leveraging the transition to net zero to gain a capital advantage.

Empirical evidence confirms this disparity. Firms in Europe with verified science-based targets have experienced an average reduction of 20.7 basis points in their cost of capital relative to their peers without such targets (Zhou et al., 2025). Yet, in Africa, Southeast Asia, and Latin America, this climate-credibility effect is largely absent. The Science Based Targets initiative (2024) reported that Africa and Latin America together account for just 4% of validated corporate science-based targets globally. This credibility gap reinforces negative investor sentiments and weakens the pricing signals needed to channel capital into low-carbon sectors. As a result, many firms in these regions face elevated interest rates, limited access to ESG financing, and low demand for green bonds.

Regional disparities in climate finance are not merely market artefacts; they stem from systemic financing distortions. According to Calcaterra et al. (2024), the average cost of capital for renewable energy projects in developing countries ranges from 7 to 10%, compared with 2–5% in advanced economies. This differential significantly undermines the affordability and bankability of decarbonisation projects in EDEs. The IEA (2024) similarly argued that high capital costs, rather than a lack of natural resources or technological maturity, are the primary bottlenecks to clean energy growth in the Global South. These financial asymmetries not only reduce firms' willingness to invest in green transitions but also delay progress towards national climate goals.

The situation in Africa illustrates the depth of this constraint. According to Wambui et al. (2023), African economies face disproportionately high transition risks due to debt burdens, limited fiscal space, and exposure to climate shocks. While central banks across the continent have begun to acknowledge these risks by joining international networks (e.g., the Network for Greening the Financial System [NGFS]), only a handful have issued regulatory guidance or developed sustainable finance taxonomies. Most African firms are exposed to volatile capital flows and foreign-denominated debt, which amplify the cost of climate-aligned borrowing. In this context, even credible corporate net-zero plans struggle to secure favourable financial terms without coordinated macro-financial reform.

Moreover, financial ecosystems in many EDEs lack the enabling infrastructure to translate climate credibility into capital gains. Unlike the EU's taxonomy-aligned finance regime or North America's climate disclosure mandates, many emerging economies do not yet require climate-related financial reporting or independent emissions verification. The Asian Development Bank (2023) found that, in Southeast Asia, the absence of mandatory disclosures hinders institutional investors from deploying capital at scale into ESG-compliant firms. As a result, local firms often rely on informal networks or state-backed banks, which typically lack the capacity or incentives to accurately price climate risk. The absence of green credit rating standards and verified disclosures increases uncertainty and raises capital costs for transition-focused firms.

To close the capital cost gap, national policymakers, central banks, and multilateral institutions must address structural barriers that distort the climate finance relationship. McKinsey & Company (2022) estimates that achieving global net-zero transition will require US$9.2 trillion annually in capital reallocation through 2050, with emerging markets accounting for the largest investment need but the weakest access. Targeted interventions (e.g., risk-sharing facilities, sovereign guarantee frameworks, concessional climate funds, and central bank participation in green bond markets) can correct these imbalances. Ultimately, the cost of capital should reflect not geography or GDP, but climate performance and transition credibility. Without such convergence, net-zero will remain a low-trust, high-cost proposition for much of the developing world.

3.8 Circular Economy Integration into Corporate Strategy

Circular economy (CE) principles have gained increasing relevance in emerging markets as firms seek to align environmental imperatives with competitive advantage. Corporate strategies adopt circular models that replace linear "take–make–dispose" systems with regenerative practices that extend product lifecycle and minimise resource use. Leading firms entrench circularity through product redesign, reverse logistics, and closed-loop manufacturing systems. Startups in India, for instance, have developed modular products with reusable components and integrated stakeholder co-creation into their value proposition, which demonstrates that even early-stage firms can institutionalise circular design (Mehrotra & Jaladi, 2022). For example, modular furniture systems developed by Indian start-ups enable easy disassembly and reuse, allowing for flexibility, affordability, and waste reduction in resource-constrained settings.

Corporate adoption of closed-loop strategies is uneven, with most firms in Latin America and the Caribbean still focused on basic end-of-life recycling. A systematic review of over 247 studies found that the region's CE activity largely revolves around recycling ("closing") rather than redesign or reuse ("narrowing" and "slowing") of product flows (Gallego-Schmid et al., 2024). More complex strategies, such as remanufacturing, repair, and regenerative design, require stronger R&D capacity, higher upfront capital, and new business models that many firms have yet to adopt. In Bogotá, Colombia, even progressive CE policies focus primarily on improving waste collection infrastructure, rather than upstream product redesign or industrial symbiosis (Rezaie et al., 2025). While such end-of-pipe approaches are necessary, they reflect a constrained institutional and technological landscape. Rezaie et al. (2025) also recommend adopting the full "10-R" framework, ranging from refuse and rethink to recover, to fully operationalise CE across value chains.

Informal workers and local entrepreneurs have become key actors in circular transitions, particularly in waste collection and material recovery. In cities such as Bogotá, informal recyclers perform critical functions in material flow, but remain excluded from corporate strategy and policy dialogue (Rezaie et al., 2025). Similarly, in parts of Africa, informal enterprises serve low-income markets by offering refurbished electronics, repurposed materials, and low-cost repair services. According to ANDE

(2024), circular SMEs across Africa face limited access to capital and fragmented regulatory support, yet continue to drive bottom-up innovations that extend product life and reduce waste. Their inclusion in formal supply chains and circular economy systems could unlock both social and environmental returns, especially in low-income urban areas.

Nevertheless, corporate integration of circular economy principles in emerging markets faces substantial structural barriers. A 2025 review by Ndoka et al. identified persistent obstacles, including high capital costs, inadequate waste management infrastructure, limited technological know-how, weak consumer awareness, and fragmented regulatory frameworks. Many firms lack access to industrial recycling parks, reverse logistics platforms, or digital systems for material tracking. Consumer preferences also remain tied to linear consumption, with a low willingness to adopt refurbished or repurposed goods. These structural deficits make it difficult for firms to scale CE models beyond the pilot initiatives or sustainability reporting.

Despite these limitations, several firms and sectors have begun integrating CE principles into their core strategies through entrepreneurial experimentation. Dantas et al. (2023) found that circular entrepreneurs in Brazil and Pakistan are motivated by both environmental motivations and cost-reduction imperatives. These firms have implemented waste-to-product systems, such as converting plastic into construction panels or producing fashion goods from textile waste. These models demonstrate that CE can be embedded not merely as a sustainability add-on, but as a primary mechanism for value creation. The success of such ventures depends on stakeholder alliances, affordable production technologies, and a clear understanding of the needs of low-income consumers.

The role of enabling institutions remains critical. In Latin America and the Caribbean, CE uptake has benefitted from a gradual shift in government policies towards bio-based industries, pollution control, and sustainable procurement (Gallego-Schmid et al., 2024). However, regulatory incentives are weak or fragmented, and CE policies often prioritise waste management over upstream innovation. More coherent policy ecosystems featuring R&D grants, tax incentives, and public–private partnerships could catalyse deeper CE integration into business models. The report by Rezaie et al. (2025) on Bogotá emphasises the importance of recognising CE as a multi-sectoral strategy that requires collaboration across government, industry, and informal actors.

3.9 Conclusion

In this chapter, we discussed the credibility, capabilities, and constraints that shape corporate transitions towards net-zero and circular economy integration in emerging markets. We highlighted significant regional and firm-level disparities in ambition, execution, and verification. While some firms have embedded low-carbon and circular principles into their core strategy (through emissions tracking, product redesign, or reverse logistics), most continue to face binding constraints linked to institutional fragility, financing barriers, as well as knowledge deficits. The RBV view helped clarify how uneven access to strategic assets (technological, human, and financial) affects firm performance in climate transitions while also revealing the organisational inertia that undermines credibility. Despite these challenges, early examples of circular entrepreneurship and blended transition strategies signal a pathway to scalable, inclusive models of corporate sustainability.

Unlocking this potential requires targeted enablers at both firm and ecosystem levels. Internally, firms must invest in climate literacy, cross-functional governance, and innovation capacity. Externally, policymakers and development partners must prioritise blended finance, public–private partnerships, and the expansion of inclusive innovation. Policy design should remain context-sensitive, avoiding one-size-fits-all frameworks and instead leveraging collaborative regulation, informal sector integration, and fiscal tools tailored to industrial structure and development stage. South-South learning (through regional alliances and peer institutions) can accelerate transitions by promoting adaptable models rather than transplanting global templates.

Future research should explore the ways in which firms operating in resource-constrained environments institutionalise sustainability while maintaining competitiveness. Longitudinal studies could examine the evolution of organisational routines, learning mechanisms, and informal actor networks under sustained decarbonisation pressures. Furthermore, there is a need to theorise how firms transition from symbolic compliance to substantive change and how the logic of the circular economy redefines firm boundaries, stakeholder relationships, and value perceptions. By embedding these inquiries within real-world constraints and institutional heterogeneity, scholars can contribute to a grounded, context-rich literature on corporate climate action in the Global South.

References

Abril, E. R. (2024). Gender and the green economy: What conditions for a gender-transformative transition to the green economy in Africa? In *Gender equality and economic development in sub-Saharan Africa* (p. 363).

African Finance Corporation. (2023). *How Africa can unlock world's most promising net-zero solution.* https://s3.eu-central-1.amazonaws.com/afc-assets/afc/AFC-Africa-Finance-Corporation-White-Paper-WEB.pdf

Ahmed, N. (2025). Empowering change through the transformative impact of women green entrepreneurs on our sustainable future. In *Empowering women through rural sustainable development and entrepreneurship* (pp. 97–120). IGI Global Scientific Publishing.

AIGCC. (2024). *High emitting companies show decarbonisation progress, stronger plans needed.* Asia Investor Group on Climate Change. https://aigcc.net/climate-action-100-net-zero-company-benchmark-2024/

ANDE. (2024). *Unlocking business opportunities in Africa's circular economy.* https://andeglobal.org/unlocking-business-opportunities-in-africas-circular-economy/

Asian Development Bank. (2023). *Asia in the global transition to net zero* (April 2023 Asian development outlook: Thematic Report). https://www.adb.org/sites/default/files/publication/876891/ado-2023-thematic-report.pdf

Asuene. (2024). *Asuene and Artemeter LLC announce strategic partnership to drive comprehensive decarbonisation solutions in Asia-Pacific.* https://asuene.com/apac/news/asuene-and-artemeter-llc-announce-strategic-partnership-to-drive-comprehensive-decarbonization-solutions-in-asia-pacific

Axon Partners Group. (2023). *Closing the climate credibility gap.* https://axonpartnersgroup.com/closing-the-climate-credibility-gap/

Bain & Company, GenZero, Standard Chartered, & Temasek. (2024). *Southeast Asia's green economy 2024: Moving the needle.* https://www.bain.com/globalassets/noindex/2024/bain_report_southeast_asias_green_economy_2024.pdf

Barney, J. (1991). Firm resources and sustained competitive advantage. *Journal of Management, 17*(1), 99–120. https://doi.org/10.1177/014920639101700108

Cahyono, P., Ramadhani, A. D., Rochmawati, I., Febriyanty, P., & Mas'ud, A. K. (2024). Leadership and ESG-based innovation (environmental, social, governance): implications for SME performance in the START-UP environment. *Journal of Contemporary Administration and Management (ADMAN), 2*(3), 591–599.

Calcaterra, M., Aleluia Reis, L., Fragkos, P., Briera, T., de Boer, H. S., Egli, F., Emmerling, J., Iyer, G., Mittal, S., Polzin, F. H. J., Sanders, M. W. J. L., Schmidt, T. S., Serebriakova, A., Steffen, B., van de Ven, D. J., van Vuuren, D. P., Waidelich, P., & Tavoni, M. (2024). Reducing the cost of capital to finance the energy transition in developing countries. *Nature Energy, 9*, 1241–1251. https://doi.org/10.1038/s41560-024-01606-7

Chan, K. J. D., Cheung, B., & Shen, L. Y. (2024). An economic foundation for assessing the credibility of corporate net zero transition pathways. *Business Strategy and the Environment*. https://doi.org/10.1002/bse.3951

Clean Air Fund. (2022). *12 cities to accelerate clean air action in Africa, Asia and Latin America*. https://www.cleanairfund.org/news-item/cities-accelerate-action-africa-asia-and-latin-america/

Climate Investment Funds. (2025). *CIF selects seven inaugural countries to pioneer industry decarbonization*. https://www.cif.org/news/IndustryCountries

Dantas, R. M., Ilyas, A., & Rita, J. X. (2023). Circular entrepreneurship in emerging markets through the lens of sustainability. *Journal of Open Innovation: Technology, Market, and Complexity, 8*(4), 211. https://doi.org/10.3390/joitmc8040211

De Haas, R., Martin, R., Muûls, M., & Schweiger, H. (2023). Managerial and financial barriers to the green transition. *SSRN Electronic Journal*. https://ssrn.com/abstract=3796559

Ferrazzi, M., & Tueske, A. (2023). *Unlocking sustainable private sector growth in the Middle East and North Africa: Small and medium enterprises in emerging economies*. World Bank. https://documents1.worldbank.org/curated/en/099920405102236971/pdf/IDU01017edd30483c04ca00b5c80a9eef01b5c7f.pdf

Gallego-Schmid, A., López-Eccher, C., Muñoz, E., Salvador, R., Cano-Londoño, N. A., Barros, M. V.,... & Guerrero, A. B. (2024). Circular economy in Latin America and the Caribbean: Drivers, opportunities, barriers and strategies. *Sustainable Production and Consumption*. https://doi.org/10.1016/j.spc.2024.09.006

GGGI. (2024). *GREENPRENEURS 2.0: Investing in climate tech startups for net-zero future. A stocktake of the Greenpreneurs initiative (2018–2023)* (Technical Report No. 35). Seoul: Global Green Growth Institute.

Hlahla, S., Goebel, A., & Hill, T. R. (2016, March). Green economy: A strategy to alleviate urban poverty and safeguard the environment? KwaZulu-Natal, South Africa. In *Urban forum* (Vol. 27, No. 1, pp. 113–127). Dordrecht: Springer Netherlands.

International Energy Agency (IEA). (2024). *Bringing down the cost of capital is key to unlocking clean energy growth in emerging economies*. https://www.iea.org/news/bringing-down-the-cost-of-capital-is-key-to-unlocking-clean-energy-growth-in-emerging-economies

International Sustainability Standards Board. (2024). *IFRS S2: Climate-related disclosures framework*. https://www.ifrs.org/issb

Kahlen, L., Moisio, M., Emmrich, J., Hagemann, M., & Roeser, F. (2021). *Climate investment in Latin America*. New Climate Institute. https://newclimate.org/sites/default/files/2021/11/2021_Annual-Investment-Report_Full-Report_Final.pdf

McKinsey & Company. (2022). *The net-zero transition: What it would cost, what it could bring*. https://www.mckinsey.com/capabilities/sustainability/our-insights/the-net-zero-transition-what-it-would-cost-what-it-could-bring

Mehrotra, S., & Jaladi, S. R. (2022). How start-ups in emerging economies embrace circular business models and contribute towards a circular economy. *Journal of Entrepreneurship in Emerging Economies, 14*(5), 727–753.

Ndoka, E., Alimehmeti, G., Shulla, K., & Voigt, B.-F. (2025). Transitioning to circular business models in developing countries: A systematic literature review of barriers, enablers, and future directions. *Discover Sustainability, 6*(605). https://doi.org/10.1007/s43621-025-01339-x

Nugraha, Y. D., Kasim, R. S. B. R., Aspiranti, T., Nurhayati, N., & Amaliah, I. (2006). How does the government boost the entrepreneurship community? In *Entrepreneurial ecosystem in higher education* (p. 8).

Paliampelou, I. (2024). Net zero targets and governance: A literature review (2009–2021). In *Handbook on corporate governance and corporate social responsibility* (pp. 49–66).

Prodanova, N., & Tarasova, O. (2024). ESG subsystems and strategies to enhance their operational efficiency. *Cadernos de Educação Tecnologia e Sociedade, 17*(1), 405–413.

PwC. (2023). *Sustainability counts: ESG insights from Asia-Pacific markets*. https://www.pwc.com/gx/en/issues/esg/esg-asia-pacific/sustainability-counts.html

Rezaie, S., Jokiaho, J., André, K., & Vanhuyse, F. (2025). *Advancing the circular economy in Latin American and Caribbean cities: evaluation of Bogotá's circular economy strategy* (SEI report). Stockholm Environment Institute. https://doi.org/10.51414/sei2025.012

Sahertian, J., Krisprimandoyo, D. A., Melinda, T., & Toreh, F. R. (2016). *Local wisdom for greenpreneurship as a solution to batik industry in Indonesia*. https://dspace.uc.ac.id/handle/123456789/825

Science Based Targets initiative (SBTi). (2024). *Monitoring report 2023*. https://files.sciencebasedtargets.org/production/files/SBTiMonitoringReport2023.pdf

Singh, R. (2025, January 10). *ESG investing in emerging markets*. ESG Beacon. https://esg-beacon.com/blogs/emerging-markets/

SLR Consulting. (2025). *SLR expands decarbonisation strategy and implementation services to Latam*. https://www.slrconsulting.com/afr/news/decarbonization-strategy-services-latam/

Tansan, B., Lang, N., Meyer, M., Gökbulut, A., Ivers, L., Hutchinson, R., Santamarta, S., Azevedo, D., & Chan, T. (2023, March 14). *The sustainability imperative in emerging markets*. Boston Consulting Group. https://www.bcg.com/publications/2023/the-importance-of-sustainability-in-business

Task Force on Climate-Related Financial Disclosures. (2023). *2023 status report on climate-related financial disclosures*. https://www.fsb-tcfd.org/reports

Tygart, W. (2025, January 12). *Emerging markets and ESG integration*. BC ESG. https://bcesg.org/business-continuity-esg-blog/emerging-markets-and-esg-integration

Wambui, R., Feyertag, J., & Monnin, P. (2023). *Net zero central banking in Africa's diverse economies: Challenges, opportunities and policy options*. Grantham Research Institute on Climate Change and the Environment, London School of Economics and Political Science. https://www.lse.ac.uk/granthaminstitute/wp-content/uploads/2023/11/Net-zero-central-banking-in-Africas-diverse-economies.pdf

Zhou, X., Williams, R., & Shrimali, G. (2025). Corporate net zero transition and financing cost: Evidence of impact from global energy and utilities sectors. *SSRN Electronic Journal*. https://doi.org/10.2139/ssrn.4957523

CHAPTER 4

Green Financing and Investment for a Sustainable Future

Abstract In this chapter, we examine how emerging markets can mobilise capital to support both green and circular economy transitions. We explore the role of financial instruments (e.g., green bonds, sustainability-linked loans, carbon markets) and institutions (e.g., development banks, regulators, regional platforms). Drawing on examples from Africa, Asia, and Latin America, we apply institutional theory to assess how regulative mandates, normative expectations, and mimetic adoption shape sustainable investment ecosystems. We identify key barriers (e.g., fragmented governance, low institutional capacity, and weak project pipelines) while outlining potential reforms that involve fintech, regional cooperation, and capacity-building initiatives.

Keywords Green finance · Sustainable investment · Emerging markets · Circular economy · Financial instruments · Institutional reform · Renewable energy · Environmental, Social and Governance (ESG)

4.1 Introduction

The transition to net-zero emissions and a circular, resource-efficient economy in emerging markets demands an unprecedented mobilisation of capital. Figure 4.1 illustrates renewable energy investments from 2014

O. Evans and O. Adeola, *Innovations in Circular Economy and Net Zero*, https://doi.org/10.1007/978-3-032-22094-3_4

to 2023, with Brazil, India, and Turkey emerging as the top three destinations for funding. However, current climate finance flows remain significantly below required levels, covering less than one-quarter of annual investment needs in regions such as Africa and South Asia (Meattle et al., 2024). Unlocking this capital is not merely a financial engineering challenge; it is fundamentally an institutional challenge. Mobilising sustainable finance at scale necessitates reforms in how capital is governed, structured, and channelled through both public and private systems. As the overshoot literature underscores, achieving climate goals is constrained less by technological limits than by institutional and governance barriers (Reisinger et al., 2025), a point that resonates with the argument that mobilising sustainable finance for emerging markets requires systemic reforms in capital governance and allocation.

Institutional theory (DiMaggio & Powell, 1983) offers a conceptual foundation for understanding how financial systems evolve in response to sustainability imperatives. It identifies three forms of institutional pressure: regulative dynamics (e.g., taxonomies, disclosure mandates), normative expectations (e.g., ESG standards, investor stewardship), and mimetic drivers (e.g., adoption of proven global models). These pressures influence how actors, from national regulators to development banks, legitimise and institutionalise green finance practices.

We apply institutional theory to examine the actors, instruments, and governance mechanisms shaping green and circular finance ecosystems. Drawing on examples from Africa, Asia, and Latin America, we identify institutional barriers and pathways for reform. Finally, we offer strategic

Country	Total Investment ($B)	Solar ($B)	Wind ($B)	Other Renewables ($B)	Rank (Top 15)
Brazil	115	64	44	7	1
India	112	73	34	5	2
Turkey	47	24	19	4	3
Vietnam	44	26	17	1	4
Chile	28	15	12	1	5
South Africa	22	15	6	1	8
Philippines	11	6	3	2	15

Fig. 4.1 Renewable energy investment by country (2014–2023) (*Data source* BloombergNEF [2024])

guidance for advancing sustainability in financial governance at both national and regional levels.

4.2 Institutional Actors: Who Drives Green Finance?

Sovereign bond investors are increasingly driving momentum for sustainable finance by prioritising climate-aligned sovereign debt instruments. Although sovereign issuers accounted for only 9% of the \$3.5 trillion thematic bond market as of September 2022, investor demand for green, social, and sustainability (GSS) bonds continues to expand (World Bank, 2022). Investors managing over \$20 trillion now integrate environmental, social, and governance (ESG) factors into sovereign credit decisions and actively seek investments that support just transitions and Paris-aligned development pathways (World Bank, 2022). Many of these investors cite impact, market diversification, and ESG integration, rather than pricing advantage, as their primary motivations. As regulators introduce stricter climate disclosure rules and shareholders intensify pressure, sovereigns are increasingly facing normative expectations to embed sustainability into their national financing strategies. In response, emerging-market governments are issuing thematic bonds to attract capital, bolster their sustainability credentials, and demonstrate institutional alignment with international goals (World Bank, 2022).

Despite growing interest, thematic bond issuance from emerging economies remains relatively modest due to persistent institutional and structural constraints. According to World Bank estimates (2022), only 15% of total thematic bonds originated from emerging markets. Key barriers include high transaction costs, technical complexities of bond structuring, and limited institutional capacity to monitor eligible expenditures. Investors also cite risks of "greenwashing", unclear project pipelines, and weak disclosure frameworks as key deterrents (World Bank, 2022). These concerns are amplified in markets with fragile institutions and low ESG ratings. For instance, five of Africa's top seven bond issuers in 2023 (e.g., Nigeria, Egypt, Kenya) were classified as high ESG risk, a classification that closely correlates with sub-investment-grade sovereign credit ratings (Sustainalytics, 2023). Importantly, this does not imply that high ESG risk prohibits issuance. Rather, it highlights the institutional credibility gaps that must be addressed to enhance investor confidence and improve pricing outcomes.

In response, green banks have emerged as purpose-built public finance institutions designed to de-risk green investments and mobilise private capital. These entities leverage public funds to provide concessional capital, first-loss guarantees, and technical support for low-carbon projects. According to Tandon et al. (2025), 51 such institutions (36 of which operate in or support emerging markets) are now part of a growing global network of climate-focused financial actors. Together, Green Bank affiliates have catalysed over USD 41 billion in sustainable investments worldwide (UNFCCC, 2018). Countries adopt various structural models depending on the institutional context. Rwanda has initiated a national green fund, the Rwanda Green Fund (FONERWA), South Africa has integrated green banking into its national development architecture, and Indonesia's PT SMI operates as a hybrid public–private platform for infrastructure finance (UNFCCC, 2018). These institutions address gaps in creditworthiness, local-currency financing, and project bankability that otherwise inhibit private capital flows into emerging economies.

Institutional theory helps explain the proliferation of green banks as both a response to global policy pressures as well as a form of mimetic adaptation. Governments adopt these models not only to fulfil climate commitments but also to emulate successful institutions (e.g., the UK Green Investment Bank or New York Green Bank) that signal credibility to markets and donors. However, the legitimacy of these entities depends on their ability to align with domestic regulatory environments, coordinate with fiscal authorities, and uphold high standards of accountability. When countries replicate foreign models without adequate contextualisation, green banks risk institutional fragility and political marginalisation. Therefore, the institutionalisation of green finance requires both alignment with global standards and adaptation to local governance structures, financial regulations, and planning cycles (Tandon et al., 2025).

National Development Banks (NDBs) are also critical actors in financing long-term, high-impact green infrastructure. These institutions operate under national mandates to address market failures, often serving as anchor investors in energy, transport, or water projects that require extended maturities or concessional terms. In Brazil, the Banco Nacional de Desenvolvimento Econômico e Social (BNDES) has played a central role in financing large-scale wind and solar projects through blended instruments and sector-specific credit lines (Green Policy Platform, 2019). In Indonesia, PT SMI has integrated ESG standards into project appraisal and supports government-aligned transition plans. Meanwhile, Nigeria's

Bank of Industry has launched green asset-backed finance facilities with support from international donors (Green Policy Platform, 2019). These examples illustrate how NDBs bridge public climate priorities with private sector execution, provided they benefit from strong governance, capital adequacy, and coherent policy mandates.

Foreign direct investment flows to utility-scale renewable energy in emerging markets by investor type from 2014 to 2023 reveal an uneven landscape (Fig. 4.2). The data reveals several notable trends. Shifting investor landscape: Project developers dominated in the early years but declined significantly after 2018, whereas commercial banks grew steadily and became the leading investors by 2023. Peak investment period: 2018 represented the peak year for both project developers (about $7.0 billion) and international utilities (about $6.0 billion). Commercial banks showed the most consistent upward trajectory, growing from approximately $1.5 billion in 2014 to about $4.5 billion in 2023. Private equity performance remained relatively stable throughout the period, exhibiting the lowest volatility among all investor types.

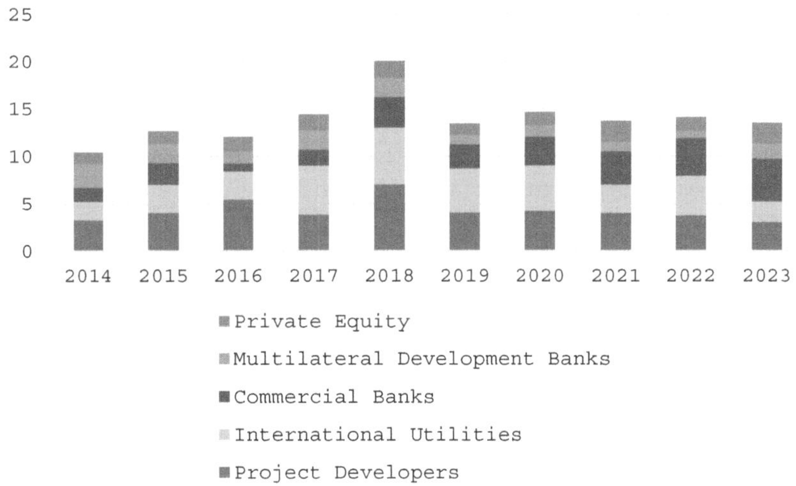

Fig. 4.2 Foreign direct investment (FDI) to utility-scale renewable energy in emerging markets, by type of investor, across the years 2014–2023 ($ billion) (*Data source* BloombergNEF [2024])

Nonetheless, institutional asymmetries across regions persist. While Latin America and Southeast Asia benefit from relatively well-capitalised and autonomous NDBs, many African NDBs are under-resourced and not fully aligned with national climate strategies (AfDB, n.d.). The African Green Bank Initiative seeks to address these institutional voids by providing technical assistance, supporting governance reforms, and establishing pooled resource platforms to scale country-level financial infrastructure. Institutional theory highlights how these efforts reflect normative convergence with international climate finance frameworks, while also underscoring the challenges of endogenous capability-building in contexts of fiscal constraint and limited state capacity. Institutionalising green finance at scale requires both global coordination and sustained national investment in institutional infrastructure.

Institutional actors (e.g., sovereign debt offices, Green Banks, NDBs) play distinct yet interdependent roles in building green finance ecosystems (Table 4.2). Sovereign debt offices attract thematic capital by signalling climate commitment; Green Banks de-risk investment and blend funding sources; and NDBs provide long-term, strategic project finance aligned with national objectives. Together, these actors form the architecture of green financial intermediation in emerging markets. Their effectiveness depends not only on capital availability but on institutional coherence, credibility, and capacity. As international pressures converge on ESG disclosure, sustainable debt standards, and green taxonomies, governments must embed these actors within broader regulatory and fiscal ecosystems to ensure systemic alignment with the climate and circular economy transitions.

4.3 Bridging Institutional and Firm-Level Perspectives: Stakeholder and Resource-Based Views

While institutional approaches explain how states, Green Banks, and national development banks (NDBs) establish enabling conditions for sustainable investment, complementary perspectives such as stakeholder theory and the resource-based view (RBV) help illuminate how firms and financial intermediaries internalise and operationalise these frameworks (Friede et al., 2015; Hart, 1995). In the context of green finance, these

Table 4.2 Institutional actors in green finance

Institution type	*Primary role*	*Regional examples*	*Institutional function*
Sovereign Bond Issuers	Raise thematic capital; signal ESG alignment	Kenya, Chile, Indonesia	Legitimise climate strategy and attract concessional debt
Green Banks	Mobilise private investment via public tools	Rwanda (FONERWA), South Africa, PT SMI (Indonesia)	De-risk projects, co-finance with the private sector
National Development Banks	Finance long-term green infrastructure	BNDES (Brazil), BOI (Nigeria), PT SMI (Indonesia)	Align finance with national development goals

perspectives highlight how organisations translate external policy incentives into strategic investment behaviour, shaping the micro-foundations of sustainability transitions.

From a stakeholder perspective, the legitimacy and effectiveness of green finance instruments depend on how well corporations and investors respond to the expectations of diverse actors (governments, creditors, shareholders, and communities) whose support is vital for sustained access to capital (Donaldson & Preston, 1995). Firms that engage transparently with stakeholders and align environmental commitments with investor preferences tend to achieve stronger reputational and financial performance (Friede et al., 2015). These dynamics underscore that sustainable finance outcomes are socially constructed through trust, accountability, and multi-actor engagement, not merely through regulatory compliance.

The resource-based view adds a complementary, capability-oriented dimension by emphasising the strategic assets that enable organisations to operationalise sustainability. The development of internal competencies (such as environmental risk assessment, sustainability reporting, and ESG data analytics) enhances firms' capacity to design, manage, and execute green investment projects effectively (Hart, 1995). Similarly, financial intermediaries that build expertise in project evaluation, impact measurement, and ESG integration can allocate capital more efficiently and reduce information asymmetries along the investment chain.

Integrating these perspectives underscores that the effectiveness of green finance ecosystems depends not only on institutional design but also on organisational capability-building and stakeholder alignment. The institutional architecture provides the framework for green finance. Still, it is the behaviour and competencies of firms, investors, and intermediaries that determine how financial instruments translate into measurable sustainability outcomes.

Figure 4.3 illustrates the multi-level drivers of green finance effectiveness, linking institutional frameworks, organisational strategies, and stakeholder outcomes. At the institutional level, policy frameworks, regulatory standards, and the operations of Green Banks and NDBs create the enabling environment for sustainable investment. The organisational level reflects how firms and financial intermediaries translate these frameworks into practice through strategic implementation: developing environmental, social, and governance (ESG) competencies, firm capabilities, and resource management systems. Finally, the stakeholder level captures the outcomes of these interactions, including sustainable investment flows, reputational gains, and long-term socio-environmental impacts. The diagram emphasises that the effectiveness of green finance depends on vertical coherence: institutional support must be matched by organisational capabilities and stakeholder engagement to generate durable, measurable sustainability outcomes.

4.4 Financial Instruments and Mechanisms

Green bonds have become an essential pillar of climate finance in emerging markets, especially in funding mitigation-oriented infrastructure (see Table 4.3). In Africa, the green bond market has grown steadily since the African Development Bank issued the continent's first bond in 2013. As of 2024, African issuers have completed 76 green bond issuances, yet the region still has less than 1% of global issuance value, just 0.3% of the $2.8 trillion global market (FSD Africa, 2025). Renewable energy dominates issuance, with solar and hydroelectric projects attracting the bulk of financing due to their scale and predictable cash flows. In contrast, adaptation-focused projects are underrepresented, with only 7% of green bond proceeds directed towards resilience outcomes. The decline in average deal sizes, from $176 million in 2013–2018 to $113 million in 2019–2024, reflects a shift from sovereign to corporate issuers but also signals potential fragmentation and a lack of scalable, bankable projects in key sectors such as agriculture and water systems (FSD Africa, 2025).

Institutional standardisation plays a critical role in the adoption of green bonds. Various frameworks (e.g., the Climate Bonds Standard,

Fig. 4.3 Multi-level drivers of green finance effectiveness

ICMA's Green Bond Principles) have established clear expectations around eligibility, reporting, and verification. However, institutional barriers remain significant in many African contexts. FSD Africa (2025) highlights persistent gaps in issuer capacity, taxonomy alignment, and impact reporting that impede investor trust. These challenges stand in sharp contrast to Asia's green bond ecosystem, where institutional maturity has translated into both scale and consistency. Between 2020 and 2024, Asia's official and corporate sectors increased their sustainable bond issuance by factors of seven and four, respectively, compared to 2015–2019 (OECD, 2025). In 2024 alone, Asian corporate issuers placed $382 billion in green bonds, while governments issued $257 billion, primarily under ICMA-compliant standards. Notably, 93% of sustainable bonds referenced external taxonomies such as the Climate Bonds Taxonomy or China's Green Taxonomy, and 81% were verified by second-party

Table 4.3 Comparative overview of green financial instruments

Instrument	*Core features*	*Leading regions/ examples*	*Key barriers to adoption*	*Institutional prerequisites*
Green bonds	Earmarked debt financing for environmental projects; proceeds tracked and reported	Asia (China, Japan); Africa (AfDB, Nigeria, Kenya); Latin America (Brazil)	Limited taxonomies; verification costs; weak adaptation-linked issuance	National green taxonomies; impact reporting systems; issuer capacity; third-party certification
Sustainability-Linked Loans (SLLs)	Performance-based loans tied to ESG KPIs; no restrictions on use of proceeds	Africa (TDB); Latin America (IFC-Colombia); Asia (India, Vietnam)	Weak ESG data infrastructure; unclear KPIs; limited verification	Borrower-level ESG tracking; performance audit systems; standardised KPIs
Multilateral Climate Funds (MCFs)	Grants or concessional loans for mitigation/ adaptation; targeted to least developed countries (LDCs)	Africa (GCF, CIF); Pacific Islands; South Asia (Bangladesh)	Long approval cycles; capacity constraints; underdeveloped project pipelines	Accredited national entities; NDC-aligned investment strategies; cross-ministerial coordination
Carbon markets	Credit-based mechanism monetising emissions reduction; traded voluntarily or in compliance markets	Africa (ACMI); Latin America (Peru, Colombia); Southeast Asia (Indonesia)	Monitoring, Reporting & Verification (MRV) gaps; benefit-sharing concerns; price volatility	Carbon registries; legal recognition of credits; community safeguards; independent verification
Cross-sectoral instruments	Blended investments across adaptation, mitigation, and development goals	Africa (cross-sectoral climate-smart agriculture, energy access)	Fragmented governance; lack of mainstreaming in national budgets	Inter-ministerial frameworks; climate-inclusive public financial management systems

opinion providers (OECD, 2025). This high degree of institutionalisation reinforces legitimacy, mitigates greenwashing concerns, and demonstrates how standard setting accelerates market development, a pattern consistent with institutional theory's emphasis on normative and mimetic convergence.

Sustainability-linked loans (SLLs) have emerged as a more flexible alternative to green bonds, particularly in markets where ESG-aligned asset pipelines are limited. Unlike green bonds, which earmark proceeds for specific uses, SLLs link financing conditions to the achievement of sustainability performance targets. These instruments offer borrowers performance-based incentives and have proven effective in unlocking climate-aligned financing in agriculture, manufacturing, as well as banking. In 2024, the Eastern and Southern African Trade and Development Bank (TDB) structured a $394 million SLL to expand climate-resilient agricultural systems, tying loan terms to measurable gender inclusion and land restoration outcomes (TDB Group, 2024). Similarly, the International Finance Corporation (IFC) extended a USD 75 million SLL to Banco Finandina in Colombia, to support SME lending for climate-smart projects (IFC, 2025). Although promising, the adoption of SLLs in Africa is slow due to weak ESG reporting infrastructure and difficulty in establishing credible, measurable KPIs. Their success depends on stronger borrower capacity, regulatory support for ESG disclosure, and clearer performance verification mechanisms.

Latin America offers a contrasting case of rapid product innovation amid institutional governance gaps. According to WWF (2025), 96% of banks in the region offer at least one green financial product, and some countries (e.g., Brazil) have pioneered Amazon-linked finance mechanisms. However, only 18% of banks implement robust ESG frameworks, and fewer than 10% have adopted net-zero targets or required nature-based safeguards (WWF, 2025). Disclosures are limited, and client-level monitoring, especially for deforestation risk, is largely absent. This disconnect between product development and institutional integration highlights an important insight: financial innovation alone cannot guarantee sustainable outcomes without accompanying governance, transparency, and accountability structures. As such, Latin America illustrates the risks of decoupling the proliferation of green finance from its foundational institutional architecture. Brazil's recent efforts to strengthen regulatory frameworks are a demonstration of a potential shift towards greater coherence, but they remain the exception rather than the norm.

Multilateral Climate Funds (MCFs) are essential for closing financing gaps, particularly for adaptation in least developed countries. In 2021/2022, MCFs provided only 2% of Africa's total climate finance, yet 81% of that support was concessional, split between grants (59%) and low-interest loans (22%) (Meattle et al., 2024). These funds primarily benefit least developed countries (LDCs), which received 74% of all MCF flows (Meattle et al., 2024). MCFs disproportionately support dual-benefit and adaptation investments in essential sectors (e.g., agriculture, water). However, procedural delays, complex eligibility criteria, and fragmented national planning processes hinder effective fund mobilisation. Many African countries lack dedicated green project pipelines or fail to integrate MCF access into national debt and investment strategies. Restructuring project approval processes, consolidating national implementation entities, and aligning investment plans with Nationally Determined Contributions (NDCs) can unlock the catalytic potential of MCFs in emerging markets.

Carbon markets represent a rapidly expanding yet inconsistently institutionalised mechanism for climate finance. Africa's proportion of global carbon credits increased significantly from 10% in 2021 to 26% in 2023, despite a plateau in global demand (UNDP, 2024). This growth is indicative of increased issuance from the land-use and energy sectors, alongside strategic initiatives such as the Africa Carbon Markets Initiative. Nonetheless, significant institutional deficiencies remain, including price volatility, inadequate benefit-sharing with local communities, and insufficient project verification frameworks, all of which undermine market credibility (FSD Africa, 2025). Disparities in project governance, transparency, and the legal recognition of carbon rights pose obstacles to achieving equitable market access. As carbon markets continue to expand, governments must implement robust legal safeguards, establish independent oversight bodies, and invest in MRV (Monitoring, Reporting, & Verification) systems to ensure both climate integrity and social inclusion. Absent institutional consolidation, carbon markets risk perpetuating power asymmetries and market opacity, particularly in nations with weak environmental governance.

4.5 Key Institutional Barriers in Emerging Markets

Emerging markets encounter entrenched institutional barriers that impede the effective mobilisation and scaling of green finance (Table 4.4). Chief among these is the absence of nationally defined, interoperable green finance taxonomies. Many jurisdictions lack clear classifications for environmentally sustainable activities, creating ambiguity in asset eligibility and undermining both issuer and investor confidence (Nguyen et al., 2024). Nguyen et al. (2024) identified the absence of green bond issuance templates and regulatory infrastructure as the most significant policy constraints in Vietnam. Without harmonised frameworks, particularly those aligned with international standards [e.g., the Climate Bonds Initiative (CBI)] or the EU Taxonomy, markets risk mislabelling assets, which invites accusations of greenwashing and discourages global investor participation. These inconsistencies hinder the development of regional green capital markets and disincentivise cross-border issuances, especially for smaller economies.

Also significant is the systemic absence of robust climate-related data systems. Many financial authorities in emerging markets lack the institutional capability to track climate risk or measure environmental impact at the asset or portfolio level. Demekas and Stallings (2023) report that most financial firms in developing economies operate without climate stress testing or mandatory ESG disclosure protocols. The situation is further complicated by the absence of harmonised indicators across ministries, regulators, and development banks. Novák et al. (2025) highlight how inconsistent data integration in BRICS and Central European economies undermines the construction of effective green financial indices. These data gaps prevent governments from designing informed fiscal incentives and hinder private actors' ability to price risk or evaluate green project pipelines accurately.

Investor confidence is fragile in many emerging markets, largely due to elevated risk premiums, currency volatility, and weak ESG enforcement. While institutional investors increasingly favour ESG-compliant assets, emerging-market green companies attract only a marginal share of global sustainable investment (de Crescenzio & Lepers, 2023). This inadequacy reflects both structural capital market biases and perceived governance risks. Wongaree et al. (2025) demonstrate that investors in the Asia-Pacific region accept lower yields on green bonds issued in local

Table 4.4 Institutional barriers to green finance in emerging markets

Barrier type	*Description*	*Key source(s)*	*Policy implication*
Regulatory taxonomy	Absence of national classification systems for green assets	Nguyen et al. (2024) and OECD (2025)	Develop harmonised taxonomies aligned to global standards
Climate risk data systems	Inadequate MRV frameworks and data integration across agencies	Novák et al. (2025) Demekas and Stallings (2023)	Invest in climate data infrastructure and ESG disclosure mandates
Investor risk perceptions	High risk premiums, ESG rating biases, FX volatility	de Crescenzio and Lepers (2023) and Wongaree et al. (2025)	Strengthen certification, risk guarantees, and currency hedging tools
Bankable project pipeline	Weak preparation capacity, limited aggregation mechanisms	OECD (2025) and Nguyen et al. (2024)	Establish national green investment facilities and technical units
Governance fragmentation	Climate finance siloed in environment ministries; poor cross-sectoral alignment	Demekas and Stallings (2023)	Integrate green finance into fiscal planning and debt strategies

currencies with robust third-party certification, a phenomenon absent in many emerging and frontier markets. Latin America offers a cautionary contrast. Despite product innovation (e.g., Amazon-linked bonds), most regional banks lack enforceable ESG frameworks and fail to require nature-related risk disclosures (WWF, 2025). The absence of comparable institutional safeguards undermines market trust, raises issuance costs, and deepens disparities between regions with similar climate vulnerabilities but divergent governance trajectories.

The persistent shortage of "bankable" green projects exacerbates capital mobilisation challenges. While governments often articulate ambitious NDCs, they struggle to translate these into investment-grade opportunities. The OECD (2025) identifies weak project preparation capacity, limited inter-agency coordination, as well as unclear revenue models as grave obstacles. A practical illustration is municipal-level climate-smart agriculture initiatives in East Africa. Despite donor interest, these projects rarely reach financial closure due to fragmented land tenure regimes, low creditworthiness of local governments, and the lack of aggregation mechanisms. Similarly, Nguyen et al. (2024) report that in Vietnam, many subnational agencies lack technical and institutional readiness to prepare compliant green bond applications. This disconnect between policy ambition and financial viability results in a shallow project pipeline, constraining deal flow in key sectors such as water, transport, and resilient agriculture.

Governance fragmentation and institutional path dependence further obstruct systemic reform. In many countries, climate finance is treated as a niche or donor-aligned function, often relegated to environmental ministries with limited budgetary control. Demekas (2023) found that most governments fail to integrate climate finance into macroeconomic planning or sovereign debt strategies, leading to duplication of efforts and inefficient fund allocation. Historical reliance on concessional finance and donor-driven planning perpetuates short-termism and weak institutional ownership. Issuers, particularly at the subnational level, often lack the skills and resources to engage with global financial markets or meet due diligence expectations, especially in contexts where bureaucratic inertia and political interference persist (Nguyen et al., 2024). These dynamics reinforce a cycle of underprepared projects, low investor uptake, and fragmented institutional responses.

From the perspective of local financial institutions, weak incentive structures and regulatory gaps further limit engagement. According to OECD (2025), financial institutions in emerging economies rarely integrate climate criteria into lending standards or risk assessments. Regulatory bodies often do not mandate ESG disclosures or apply capital-weighting to green loans. As a result, banks treat sustainable lending as peripheral rather than strategic. Demekas and Stallings (2023) emphasised that in the absence of credit guarantees, tax incentives, or green securitisation frameworks, private finance will remain risk-averse and reactive. This inadequacy is particularly damaging in markets where banks control the majority of domestic capital but face no regulatory or reputational pressure to support green sectors. Without targeted interventions, this institutional inertia prevents the reallocation of capital towards climate-aligned development goals.

Institutional reform in emerging markets often proceeds slowly due to entrenched administrative legacies and complex political economy dynamics. Many developing countries inherited rigid budgeting systems and sector-specific financial structures shaped by donor priorities or commodity-driven growth models. Novák et al. (2025) conclude that aligning green finance with inclusive financial development goals requires not only technical innovation but also institutional realignment as well as peer benchmarking. Institutional theory suggests that reforms take hold when new norms are both politically legitimate and operationally embedded. As discussed in the later sections, bridging these structural and normative gaps will require coordinated reform across fiscal policy, public investment planning, and financial regulation to mainstream climate finance and close the institutional confidence deficit.

4.6 Policy Frameworks and International Cooperation

National policy frameworks shape the architecture and credibility of sustainable finance across emerging markets. Nigeria exemplifies this trajectory through its issuance of Africa's first sovereign green bond in 2017, followed by regulatory enhancements supported by the Securities and Exchange Commission and Financial Sector Deepening Africa (FSD Africa) (FSD Africa, 2025). India's policy model combines Reserve Bank of India guidelines with a sovereign green bond framework aligned with the ICMA Green Bond Principles, thereby bolstering investor confidence. Brazil has strengthened ESG oversight through disclosure mandates targeting banks and asset managers, particularly those offering Amazon-linked instruments (WWF, 2025). In contrast, Vietnam illustrates the risks of underdeveloped frameworks: despite having a national climate strategy, its lack of standardised green bond issuance templates and subnational capacity limit market uptake (Nguyen et al., 2024). Meanwhile, Chile has pioneered sovereign sustainability-linked bonds (SLBs) directly tied to its NDCs, making it one of the few countries to insert conditionality into sovereign financing (OECD, 2025). These cases reveal how policy coherence, institutional readiness, and fiscal innovation combine to shape domestic green finance ecosystems.

International organisations are major enablers of the development of green finance through technical guidance, capacity-building, and normative frameworks. The World Bank has supported emerging markets in integrating ESG factors into sovereign debt instruments and has assisted debt management offices in designing climate-aligned bond frameworks (Demekas & Stallings, 2023). UNDP has mobilised technical assistance across Africa via the Africa Carbon Markets Initiative (ACMI), which facilitates project verification, carbon pricing mechanisms, and national strategy development (UNDP, 2024). The OECD has produced key policy frameworks aimed at harmonising taxonomy design, sustainable disclosure standards, and fiscal incentives (OECD, 2025). The G20 Sustainable Finance Working Group has further promoted regulatory coherence by advancing interoperability between national and international green taxonomies. These multilateral actors enable countries to institutionalise climate finance tools while also mitigating fragmentation across jurisdictions and capital markets.

Policy synchronisation across ministries, central banks, and regulators is a vital precondition for the effective mobilisation of sustainable finance. OECD (2025) emphasises that many countries still treat green finance as an environmental issue rather than integrating it into macroeconomic management. Vietnam illustrates this disconnect: although national climate targets exist, subnational agencies face challenges in preparation of credible and certifiable green bond applications due to limited procedural guidance and cross-agency cooperation (Nguyen et al., 2024). In contrast, Chile's Ministry of Finance coordinates climate budget tagging, investor roadshows, and debt sustainability planning, resulting in a coherent investment narrative for both domestic and international actors. Such examples underscore how cross-ministerial cooperation, supported by statutory mandates and budgetary tools, enhances national credibility and improves the scale and quality of green finance flows.

Technical assistance and disclosure reform are equally essential components of the institutional infrastructure of sustainable finance. Without standardised impact metrics, third-party verification, or transparent reporting protocols, green instruments risk investor scepticism and accusations of greenwashing. FSD Africa (2025) has called for more rigorous data systems to validate green bond allocations in African markets. Similarly, Demekas and Stallings (2023) show that most financial institutions in low- and middle-income countries lack both the tools and incentives to integrate climate-adjusted risk metrics into credit assessments. The World Bank and UNDP have responded with targeted support, offering grant-based assistance for ESG scoring systems, climate tagging, and sovereign debt alignment. These interventions are particularly critical in fiscally constrained environments, where institutional maturity lags behind climate ambition.

From an institutional theory lens, the uptake of green finance frameworks in emerging markets reflects broader patterns of norm diffusion and transnational pressure. As global finance shifts towards ESG integration, emerging markets increasingly emulate standards set by dominant actors (e.g., the EU, ICMA, the Climate Bonds Initiative). This mimetic isomorphism is evident in the growing convergence around disclosure standards, green taxonomies, and verification procedures (OECD, 2025; Wongaree et al., 2025). Nigeria's adoption of ICMA-aligned green bond principles and Brazil's new ESG supervisory mandates both illustrate how perceived legitimacy and peer benchmarking motivate policy convergence. Yet, this diffusion process is not solely top-down. Regional platforms (e.g., the ASEAN Capital Markets Forum, the African Green Finance Coalition, and the Community of Latin American and Caribbean States [CELAC]) facilitate horizontal learning and South–South policy exchange. These platforms help adapt international standards to domestic contexts, mitigating the risk of misfit or tokenistic adoption.

Finally, international cooperation must evolve from rule-setting to collaborative problem-solving. Many emerging markets are wary of externally imposed frameworks that lack sensitivity to local constraints, political economy dynamics, or capacity asymmetries. OECD (2025) advocates for participatory models of global finance governance that include subnational authorities, local financial institutions, and non-state actors. Policy transfer must shift from blueprint replication to co-creation, an approach that acknowledges differentiated capabilities and climate vulnerabilities. As sustainable finance transitions from voluntary to mandatory regimes, multilateral actors must ensure that frameworks empower rather than burden emerging markets. Future efforts should focus on building institutional legitimacy, not just procedural compliance, to ensure that global financial norms translate into equitable and scalable green investment.

4.7 Pathways Forward: Strengthening Green Finance Ecosystems

Strengthening national green finance ecosystems demands sustained capacity-building for NDBs and financial regulators (see Fig. 4.4). Many emerging market institutions still lack the technical capabilities to assess climate risks, integrate ESG criteria, and structure innovative green instruments. Demekas and Stallings (2023) observed that regulatory agencies in low- and middle-income countries often operate with minimal climate-related supervisory guidance. Nguyen et al. (2024) further reported that even when frameworks exist, many subnational and public-sector actors struggle to translate them into bankable instruments due to weak technical training alongside procedural ambiguity. As such, international cooperation should prioritise diagnostic capacity-building missions, ESG impact reporting systems, as well as targeted knowledge transfer to NDBs and financial authorities tasked with implementing climate-aligned mandates.

Regional platforms offer a compelling opportunity to address market fragmentation and facilitate pooled green investment. In smaller economies or those with limited sovereign issuance capacity, joint investment platforms can aggregate demand, spread transaction costs, as well as facilitate cross-border standardisation. The ASEAN Capital Markets Forum and the African Green Finance Coalition are early efforts to harmonise green bond principles and share verification infrastructure. OECD (2025) emphasises the need for multilateral support to help these regional platforms function as intermediaries between local issuers and global capital. By building common taxonomies, technical standards, and rating approaches, regional bodies can enhance investor confidence while deepening the liquidity and maturity of local green capital markets.

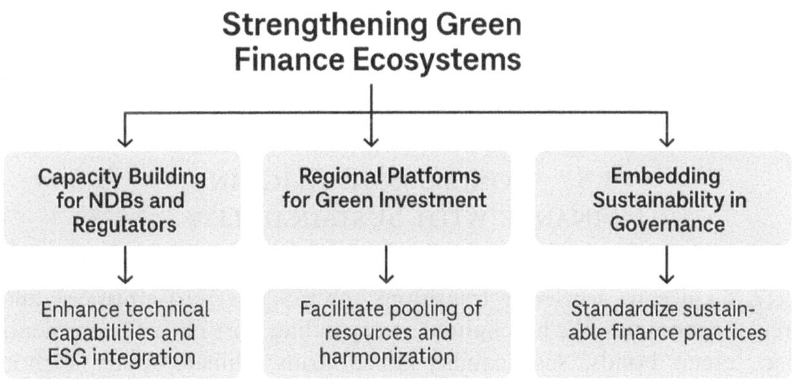

Fig. 4.4 Pathway forward for green finance ecosystems

Digital innovation and green fintech constitute a largely untapped yet transformative enabler of investment transparency and tracking. Blockchain applications can enhance the traceability of green bond proceeds, while AI-powered ESG scoring systems can automate disclosure validation. The UNDP (2024) notes that many carbon market registries in Africa are currently piloting digital MRV systems to streamline credit issuance and reduce verification costs. Similarly, the OECD (2025) advocates for the digital tagging of public budgets and investment pipelines to identify climate-aligned spending and facilitate real-time auditing. Demekas (2023) observes that most emerging market regulators lack access to such tools, thereby undermining their ability to monitor compliance and assess systemic climate-related financial risks. Investing in green fintech infrastructure can significantly improve transparency, reduce transaction friction, and build trust in underdeveloped markets.

The institutionalisation of sustainability in financial governance requires more than procedural upgrades; it demands the entrenchment of environmental goals into the normative structures and mandates of financial institutions (Table 4.5). Novák et al. (2025) propose composite indicators that capture both financial inclusion and environmental performance as tools for monitoring systemic progress. This aligns with institutional theory's insight that norms become entrenched when reinforced by peer expectations, supervisory mandates, and reputational incentives. Wongaree et al. (2025) demonstrate that green bond certification, credit ratings, and currency hedging mechanisms reduce perceived issuer risk, thereby encouraging policy replication. As regulators, central banks, and NDBs internalise sustainability as a fiduciary obligation, rather than an externality, green finance practices will increasingly shape financial sector governance across emerging markets.

4.8 Conclusion: Aligning Finance with Sustainability

In this chapter, we have examined how emerging markets can harness green finance to accelerate transitions towards net-zero emissions and circular economies. We highlighted an expanding portfolio of instruments (e.g., green bonds, sustainability-linked loans, climate funds, carbon markets). We explored the institutional actors, from sovereign debt managers to green banks and NDBs, who mediate access to capital and drive financial innovation. However, tools alone do not generate systemic

Table 4.5 Finance–policy checklist for policymakers in emerging markets

Priority area	*Strategic action points*
Regulatory frameworks	Develop national green taxonomies and embed ESG disclosures within prudential regulation and sovereign bond frameworks
Institutional capacity	Equip NDBs, central banks, and regulators with tools for ESG integration, climate risk modelling, and project pipeline preparation
Private capital mobilisation	Launch Green Banks or blended finance vehicles to co-invest with private capital and de-risk climate infrastructure investments
Climate fund access	Establish in-country climate finance units to structure proposals, manage compliance, and ensure transparent reporting to entities like GCF and CIF
Carbon market readiness	Deploy digital MRV systems and national carbon registries; create legal frameworks for credit issuance and community benefit-sharing
Regional coordination	Participate in regional sustainable finance coalitions (e.g., the ASEAN Capital Markets Forum and the African Green Finance Coalition) to facilitate pooled issuance and capacity exchange
Digital innovation & fintech	Invest in green fintech platforms that support traceability (e.g., blockchain), automated ESG scoring, and real-time tracking of investment impact

impact; their effectiveness depends on the institutional environments in which they operate.

Persistent challenges (e.g., weak taxonomies, limited technical capacity, fragmented regulatory mandates) continue to undermine trust and impede scale. Tackling these barriers requires more than isolated reforms. As institutional theory reminds us, sustainable transformation occurs when norms, expectations, and mandates evolve together. Regulatory coherence, credible disclosure systems, and mission-driven institutions must form the foundation of green financial systems. Equally important are localised innovation, tailored ESG frameworks, regional investment platforms, and digital MRV tools that align with domestic priorities while interoperating with global standards.

Looking ahead, policymakers must transcend the superficial labelling of financial products and focus on designing robust green financial ecosystems. These ecosystems should integrate sustainability into the mandates of central banks, fiscal strategies, and capital market infrastructure. Regional coalitions and South–South platforms are expected to play a pivotal role in establishing shared principles, consolidating projects, and formulating standards. National Development Banks (NDBs) and financial regulators should not merely function as intermediaries; rather, they should act as system architects, steering the financial sector towards a just, inclusive, and climate-resilient future.

References

African Development Bank. (n.d.). *African Green Banks Initiative*. https://www.afdb.org/en/topics-and-sectors/initiatives-and-partnerships/african-green-banks-initiative

BloombergNEF. (2024). *Climatescope 2024: Emerging Markets Power Factbook*. Available at: https://www.global-climatescope.org/downloads/climatescope-emerging-markets-power-factbook-2024.pdf

de Crescenzio, A., & Lepers, E. (2023, October 30). *The lack of portfolio investment finance in green companies in emerging markets*. VoxEU. https://cepr.org/voxeu/columns/lack-portfolio-investment-finance-green-companies-emerging-markets

Demekas, D. (2023, November 29). *Green finance in emerging markets: A ground-level view*. OMFIF. https://www.omfif.org/2023/11/green-finance-in-emerging-markets-a-ground-level-view/

Demekas, D., & Stallings, J. A. (2023). *Challenges of green finance—Private sector perspectives from emerging markets*. World Bank. http://documents.worldbank.org/curated/en/099717411212328052

DiMaggio, P. J., & Powell, W. W. (1983). The iron cage revisited: Institutional isomorphism and collective rationality in organizational fields. *American Sociological Review, 48*(2), 147–160. https://doi.org/10.2307/2095101

Donaldson, T., & Preston, L. E. (1995). The stakeholder theory of the corporation: Concepts, evidence, and implications. *Academy of Management Review, 20*(1), 65–91.

FSD Africa. (2025). *Impact of green bonds in Africa*. https://fsdafrica.org/wp-content/uploads/2025/05/Green-Bond-Report_Final-report-20.03.2025.pdf

Friede, G., Busch, T., & Bassen, A. (2015). ESG and financial performance: Aggregated evidence from more than 2000 empirical studies. *Journal of Sustainable Finance & Investment, 5*(4), 210–233.

Green Policy Platform. (2019). *Financing climate futures: The role of national development banks in Brazil and South Africa*. https://www.greenpolicyplatform.org/case-studies/financing-climate-futures-role-national-development-banks-brazil-and-south-africa

Hart, S. L. (1995). A natural-resource-based view of the firm. *Academy of Management Review, 20*(4), 986–1014.

IFC. (2025). *IFC announces sustainability-linked loan of up to US$75 million for Banco Finandina in Colombia*. https://www.ifc.org/en/pressroom/2025/ifc-announces-sustainability-linked-loan-of-up-to-us-75-million-for-banco-finandin

Meattle, C., Balm, A., Diaz, J. E., Miao, G., Stout, S., Gupta, I., Abraham, S., Sloley, A., & Wignarajah, D. (2024). *Landscape of climate finance in Africa 2024*. Climate Policy Initiative. https://www.climatepolicyinitiative.org/publication/landscape-of-climate-finance-in-africa-2024/

Nguyen, P.-H., Nguyen, L.-A.T., Le, H.-Q., & Tran, L.-C. (2024). Navigating critical barriers for green bond markets using a fuzzy multi-criteria decision-making model: Case study in Vietnam. *Heliyon, 10*(13), e33493. https://doi.org/10.1016/j.heliyon.2024.e33493

Novák, Z., Fáth, G., Ge, C., & Kumar, P. (2025). Inclusive green finance: An approach for developing a comprehensive indicator for BRICS and other emerging economies. *Journal of Economic Structures, 14*(1), 10. https://doi.org/10.1186/s40008-025-00354-5

OECD. (2025a). *Mobilising private finance for development, climate and biodiversity in emerging markets and developing economies: Financing our futures* (Business and Finance Policy Papers No. 91). https://doi.org/10.1787/ada2dfcd-en

OECD. (2025b). Sustainable bonds. In *Asia Capital Markets Report 2025*. https://www.oecd.org/en/publications/asia-capital-markets-report-2025_02172cdc-en/full-report/sustainable-bonds_21e9a353.html

Reisinger, A., Fuglestvedt, J. S., Pirani, A., Geden, O., Jones, C. D., Maharaj, S.,... & Seneviratne, S. I. (2025). Overshoot: A conceptual review of exceeding and returning to global warming of 1.5 °C. *Annual Review of Environment and Resources, 50*.

Sustainalytics. (2023). *ESG Spotlight | New Frontiers: African Sovereign Debt and ESG Risk*. https://connect.sustainalytics.com/esg-spotlight-african-sovereign-debt-and-esg-risk

Tandon, G., Mitra, D., Khanna, N., First, J., & Buchner, B. (2025). *The State of Green Banks 2025: Learnings from green financing structures around the world*. Climate Policy Initiative. https://www.climatepolicyinitiative.org/publication/the-state-of-green-banks-2025

TDB Group. (2024). *Landmark USD 394 million sustainability-linked loan to boost African agriculture*. https://www.tdbgroup.org/landmark-usd-394-million-sustainability-linked-loan-to-boost-african-agriculture/

s

UNDP. (2024). *Carbon markets in Africa: Balancing finance mobilisation with emission reduction goals*. https://www.undp.org/africa/blog/carbon-markets-africa-balancing-finance-mobilization-emission-reduction-goals

UNFCCC. (2018). *Green Bank Network mobilises $41 billion for clean energy projects around the globe*. https://unfccc.int/news/green-bank-network-mobilizes-us41-billion-for-clean-energy-projects-around-the-globe

Wongaree, P., Chiyachantana, C. N., Ding, D. K., Prasarnphanich, P., & Siwasarit, W. (2025). The pricing of green bonds and the determinants of the green bond premium in the Asia-Pacific and European markets. 11(2), 100546. https://doi.org/10.1016/j.joitmc.2025.100546

World Bank. (2022). *Sovereign green, social and sustainability bonds: Unlocking the potential for emerging markets and developing economies*. https://thedocs.worldbank.org/en/doc/4de3839b85c57eb958dd207fad132f8e-0340012022/original/WB-GSS-Bonds-Survey-Report.pdf

WWF. (2025). *Banks in Africa and Latin America can lead green growth and transition*. https://wwf.panda.org/?13985416/Banks-in-Africa-and-Latin-America-can-lead-green-growth-and-transition

CHAPTER 5

Circular Economy in Food Systems and Urban Development

Abstract In this chapter, we examine the institutional, technological, and governance challenges that impede the adoption of circular economy practices in food and urban systems across emerging economies. We analyse how regulatory fragmentation, cultural norms, and informality hinder circular economy strategies, including food reuse, waste segregation, and low-emission agriculture. Applying institutional theory and the diffusion of innovation framework, we highlight the need for modular technologies, inclusive policies, and localised capacity-building. We conclude with recommendations for harmonised regional frameworks and multi-scalar approaches to enable equitable and scalable transitions to the circular economy in resource-constrained environments.

Keywords Circular economy · Food systems · Urban development · Emerging economies · Institutional barriers · Regenerative agriculture · Policy fragmentation · Waste management

5.1 Introduction

Circular economy strategies within food and urban systems present substantial opportunities to mitigate environmental degradation, alleviate food insecurity, and enhance resource efficiency (Albaladejo et al.,

O. Evans and O. Adeola, *Innovations in Circular Economy and Net Zero*, https://doi.org/10.1007/978-3-032-22094-3_5

2023; Marrero et al., 2022; UNDP, 2024). In emerging economies, these systems contribute disproportionately to waste, emissions, and resource depletion, driven by factors such as urbanisation, informal markets, and infrastructural deficits (Marrero et al., 2022; UNDP, 2024). Figure 5.1 shows that among emerging-market cities, Dubai, Buenos Aires, and Quezon City have achieved the highest overall circular economy performance, with strong scores across all three pillars: circular buildings, circular living, and circular procurement. In contrast, cities such as Lagos and Nairobi exhibit significant gaps, particularly in circular buildings and procurement initiatives. The rapid urban growth in cities like Lagos and Manila places considerable strain on waste management systems, while increasing food demand exacerbates ecological pressures across supply chains (Oladosu et al., 2024; Sicam, 2023). Furthermore, the effectiveness of circular economy initiatives in emerging markets is inextricably linked to broader economic dynamics, as rising energy prices, although often perceived as a threat to competitiveness, can also drive innovation and efficiency gains among firms (Calì et al., 2023).

Institutional and behavioural constraints continue to impede the adoption of circular economy practices. Informality dominates food and waste logistics across Sub-Saharan Africa and Latin America (AGRA, 2021), while regulatory fragmentation hinders surplus recovery and material reuse (Aguilar et al., 2024; Nutrition Connect, 2023). Cultural norms

Fig. 5.1 Urban performance on circular economy pillars: comparative indicators across emerging market cities (*Data source* Bloomberg [2025])

and aspirational consumption further reinforce linear patterns, particularly in dietary preferences shaped by rising incomes (Marrero et al., 2022). In this chapter, we apply institutional theory and the diffusion of the innovation framework to analyse these barriers. Institutional theory clarifies how coercive, mimetic, and normative dynamics shape regulatory behaviour and professional inertia, while diffusion theory explains variation in the uptake of circular economy technologies, particularly across fragmented, low-literacy environments.

5.2 Institutional Barriers to Circular Food Systems

Circular economy approaches are underutilised in food systems across the Global South, primarily due to institutional constraints that restrict regulatory coherence, cultural alignment, financial inclusion, and market integration. These barriers intersect across formal and informal domains, reinforcing systemic inertia, which limits the adoption of circular practices.

In India, food waste remains significant despite institutional efforts. Approximately one-third of all food in the country is spoilt or wasted before consumption (Nutrition Connect, 2023). While the Food Safety and Standards Authority of India (FSSAI) has launched the "Save Food, Share Food" initiative to facilitate the safe donation of surplus food, its implementation suffers from fragmented coordination. Municipal authorities lack enforcement mechanisms and inter-agency protocols to support redistribution logistics. Liability concerns among donors, the absence of insurance schemes, and unclear safety guidelines further discourage participation from food businesses and retailers. Although the FSSAI promotes a culture of sustainable consumption under its "Eat Right India" campaign, local governments and private stakeholders have not uniformly adopted these standards, reflecting policy gaps and operational fragmentation (Nutrition Connect, 2023).

In Latin America, cultural norms of food consumption undermine circular food transitions. Studies reveal a consistent shift from traditional, plant-based diets towards meat-heavy, ultra-processed consumption patterns, often perceived as symbols of affluence and modernity (Marrero et al., 2022). Although meat accounts for just 7.5–12.7% of dietary intake across the region, it contributes to over 70% of food-related greenhouse gas emissions and more than half of the associated land and water use (Marrero et al., 2022). These patterns suggest that circular economy-compatible dietary shifts (e.g., revalorising legumes, roots, and traditional grains) face resistance rooted in socio-cultural identity and consumer aspirations. Public policy often fails to actively promote such alternatives, allowing informal food cultures to dominate without institutional support.

In Sub-Saharan Africa, regenerative agriculture presents a compelling model for circularity through improvements in soil health, erosion reduction, and biodiversity. However, institutional and economic obstacles have inhibited its adoption. High upfront labour requirements, lack of financial incentives, as well as limited access to knowledge or extension services deter smallholders from implementing these practices (Africa Regenerative Agriculture Study Group, 2021). Although some organisations (for example, Nespresso and Olam) have reported yield increases of between 68 and 300% through regenerative methods, these successes remain donor-driven and disconnected from national agricultural frameworks (Kabiri, 2024). Moreover, the region applies only 22 kg of fertiliser per hectare (far below the global average of 146 kg), illustrating input constraints that further marginalise circular economy-compatible farming (Kabiri, 2024). Despite evidence of potential returns of USD 5–30 per dollar invested in regenerative approaches, governments rarely embed such models in formal extension systems or financing schemes (Kabiri, 2024).

Market informality also constrains circular adoption. Across African and Latin American cities, more than 80% of food is traded through informal markets (AGRA, 2021). These systems operate outside traceability regimes, hygiene regulations, and material recovery infrastructure, thereby complicating their integration into circular economy supply chains. Vendors often lack access to cooling, composting, or redistribution platforms, and attempts to formalise their operations frequently impose unrealistic compliance demands (AGRA, 2021). As a result, informal actors are peripheral to national circular strategies despite playing a central role in local food systems.

Institutional theory helps explain the persistence of these barriers. Coercive isomorphism arises when donor organisations introduce international circular economy frameworks that clash with local market realities, particularly in under-resourced municipalities. Mimetic isomorphism occurs when governments replicate high-tech circular economy models from Europe without the requisite infrastructure readiness. Normative barriers manifest in the lack of training on circular economy principles for agricultural extension agents, urban planners, and local food inspectors, leaving critical implementers unaware of circular economy options (Challa, 2025; Kabiri, 2024). Overcoming these institutional bottlenecks requires regulatory integration, cultural reorientation, and inclusive policy tools that recognise informal actors and region-specific knowledge systems as legitimate contributors to circular economy transitions.

5.3 Technology Diffusion in Food Systems

Circular economy technologies can improve food system sustainability in low and middle-income countries. However, unequal access to information, finance, infrastructure, and institutional support continues to hinder their widespread adoption. The Diffusion of Innovation theory is a valuable lens for analysing how early adopters navigate structural constraints and how reinvention (local adaptation of technologies) can influence successful implementation across diverse contexts.

In Vietnam, a pioneering initiative under the "One Million Hectares" program illustrates circular economy-aligned technology diffusion in rice production. Farmers adopted certified seeds, direct-seeded mechanisation, alternate wetting and drying techniques, and rice straw-based innovations to improve both environmental outcomes and profits. Compared with traditional broadcast methods, pilot farms using these techniques reported yield increases of 5.8–6.5 tonnes per hectare and reduced greenhouse gas emissions by more than 2 tonnes CO_2-eq/ha. Profits increased by approximately USD 200 per hectare (IRRI, 2024). The Vietnamese Ministry of Agriculture and the International Rice Research Institute (IRRI) attribute these results to collaborative governance, integrated value-chain management, and the use of rice straw in circular bio-economy practices (UNDP, 2024).

In Nigeria, post-harvest losses are a critical challenge. Approximately 35–45% of fresh produce (valued at up to USD 4 billion annually) is lost due to inadequate cold storage and transport systems (Okojie, 2023). In response, Nigerian start-up Ecotutu launched a solar-powered cold chain solution in Lagos's Mile 12 market, the country's largest fresh produce hub. Its pay-as-you-chill model leverages IoT-based monitoring for temperature control and energy efficiency, enabling small-scale retailers to access affordable storage services without major capital investment.

This decentralised cooling infrastructure demonstrates how modular technologies tailored to informal market dynamics can reduce spoilage while boosting market resilience.

Kenya demonstrates how low-cost digital solutions can support climate-resilient agriculture through the reinvention of circular economy technologies. The UNFCCC-supported agro-weather tool disseminates real-time alerts via SMS, radio, and computers to smallholder farmers in semi-arid regions. Using this tool, about 5,000 households have adopted adaptive practices and water-saving techniques that reduce crop losses from erratic rainfall. Over 80% of participating households now utilise existing woodlots for carbon sequestration, thereby avoiding deforestation for fuel (UNFCCC, 2024). Such initiatives exemplify reinvention: the integration of agronomic modelling with accessible communication methods increases the diffusion of technology beyond digitally literate users.

In India, digital extension services are unevenly distributed across gender and socio-economic lines. A study conducted in Telangana found that 81% of rural female farmers lack consistent Internet access, while 70% have limited training in operating digital tools (Challa, 2025). Constraints include dual household-agricultural responsibilities, low e-readiness, and cost barriers to smartphone ownership. These factors collectively marginalise female farmers from participating in tech-driven circular food systems (Challa, 2025). The exclusion of this significant demographic group from early adoption cycles hinders systemic transformation and perpetuates inequality in access to digital innovation.

Across these cases, several patterns emerge (Table 5.1). First, innovators and early adopters often rely on strong institutional partnerships (e.g., public–private or NGO-supported pilots). Second, reinvention is critical: Vietnam's integration of rice straw reuse, Kenya's use of SMS-radio hybrids, and Nigeria's context-specific storage models all reveal that technological diffusion benefits from local customisation. Third, systemic gaps in digital infrastructure and training, particularly among women and informal actors, remain persistent barriers that require targeted interventions.

The Diffusion of Innovation theory underscores that technology does not spread linearly. Adoption depends on factors such as relative advantages, compatibility with cultural and economic conditions, ease of use, trialability, and observability. In the Global South, these variables often rely not only on technical merit but also on institutions' capacity

Table 5.1 Technology diffusion in food systems

Country	*Technology or innovation*	*Circular economy function*	*Enabler*	*Barrier*	*Reinvention or diffusion insight*
Vietnam	Mechanised direct-seeded rice, rice straw reuse	Low-emission farming, waste reuse	Ministry of Agriculture, IRRI, certified seed networks	Infrastructure gap in non-pilot areas	Integrated rice straw circularity model with yield boost
Nigeria	Solar-powered cold chain (Ecotutu)	Post-harvest loss reduction	Private sector innovation, pay-as-you-chill model	High produce spoilage rates; informal market volatility	Modular tech aligns with informal vendor needs
Kenya	SMS/radio agro-weather alerts	Climate resilience, resource efficiency	Public climate tools, multichannel info delivery	Limited mobile access in arid regions	Reinvented digital tool via radio for low-connectivity areas
India	Digital extension services for women farmers	Knowledge dissemination, inclusion barrier	Government/ NGO platforms (partial reach)	Low literacy, dual labour roles, and limited device ownership	Highlights digital gender divide in circular economy tech access

to support inclusive innovation ecosystems. Therefore, future circular economy transitions must prioritise contextual reinvention and systemic inclusion to foster equitable technology uptake.

5.4 Urban Circular Economy: Institutional Hurdles

Figure 5.2 shows that Dubai and Buenos Aires lead in recycling practices, with strong performance across all three waste categories, while cities such as Lagos and Nairobi demonstrate significant gaps in waste recycling infrastructure, particularly in water and construction waste management. The implementation of an urban circular economy in emerging cities is hindered by persistent institutional barriers rooted in fragmented governance, inadequate planning frameworks, and unresolved tensions

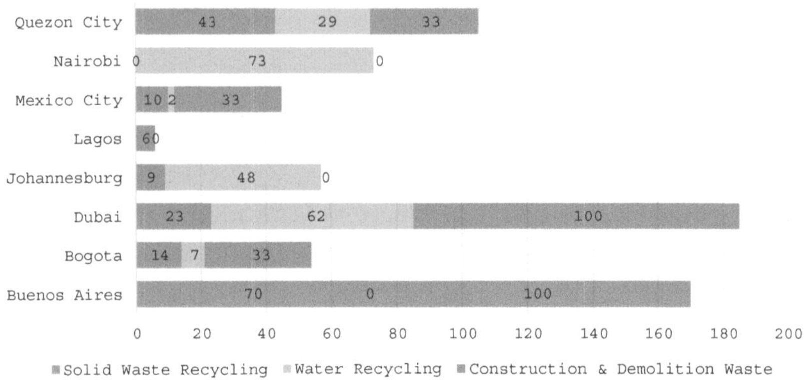

Fig. 5.2 Recycling practices in urban waste management: solid, water, and construction waste across cities (*Data source* Bloomberg [2025])

between formal and informal actors. These constraints manifest in operational failures, weak regulatory coherence, and limited capacity to absorb innovation, despite rising waste generation and environmental stress.

In Lagos, the absence of formal waste segregation policies and incentives has contributed to widespread operational inefficiency in municipal waste management. Despite the state's population exceeding 20 million and the generation of thousands of tonnes of waste daily, Lagos lacks a unified waste segregation protocol and sufficient sanitary landfills (Oladosu et al., 2024). Government agencies have adopted fragmented strategies, often limited to temporary interventions that do not address the root causes. Most residents lack access to collection services and dispose of waste indiscriminately. Oladosu et al. (2024) found that the city has failed to adopt a comprehensive collection and recycling strategy or any functional framework for public cooperation. These shortcomings stem from administrative fragmentation, poor enforcement of environmental laws, and inadequate budget allocation. Civil society engagement remains limited, and CE-aligned practices such as composting and decentralised recycling remain marginal.

In Manila, informal recycling economies occupy a vital yet precarious position within the urban system. Waste pickers in Tondo Bay contribute significantly to material recovery and recycling by operating informal facilities in residential areas (Sicam, 2023). However, municipal zoning laws do not recognise their spatial or economic contributions. Formal urban planning approaches, rooted in modernist ideals, have marginalised these actors and overlooked the productive role they play in the sustenance of low-cost, decentralised circular economy infrastructure. Sicam (2023) observed that these waste pickers co-produce a unique urban morphology in which residential and commercial uses intersect informal recycling networks. Yet, policymakers have overlooked their agency and instead prioritised redevelopment plans that displace them without offering compensation or integration. The city continues to operate under a dual system (formal infrastructure planning and informal circular economy labour) without creating a pathway for institutional reconciliation.

Governance weaknesses also impede public–private collaboration in circular economy infrastructure development, particularly in waste and water services. In South Asia, fragmented municipal governance has obstructed the development of waste-to-energy (WtE) systems, with Bangladesh, India, and Pakistan failing to reach scale despite their strong potential (Amin et al., 2023). Amin et al. (2023) attribute this failure to the absence of cooperative environmental governance and the exclusion of local communities from decision-making processes. Similarly, in water and sanitation, cities have adopted public–private partnerships (PPPs) without establishing performance-based contracting or accountability mechanisms. In Lagos, the state has not prioritised waste utility reform, and PPPs remain underdeveloped despite external donor support (Oladosu et al., 2024). In contrast, some cities in Southeast Asia, such as Ho Chi Minh City, have implemented PPPs to reduce non-revenue water through targeted leakage contracts, achieving substantial gains in efficiency (World Bank, 2023).

Path dependency theory offers insights into why many urban planning systems are incompatible with a circular economy. Schindler and Dionisio (2021) note that decision support tools (DSTs) often reinforce existing car-centric and linear planning paradigms. In their analysis of urban planning, they showed that DSTs embedded historical design logic into new planning decisions, thereby limiting innovation. In many emerging cities, planners continue to replicate models focused on large-scale infrastructure, private transport, and centralised waste disposal, choices that diverge sharply from decentralised, regenerative urban models. Recognising the embeddedness of these planning cultures is essential to designing policies that disrupt legacy systems and promote circular economy-compatible outcomes. To advance an urban circular economy, cities must dismantle these institutional path dependencies. Reform requires multi-sectoral coordination, legal recognition of informal systems, and performance-based partnerships grounded in clear accountability. Without these reforms, circular economy transitions will remain aspirational rather than operational.

Promote circular economy-compatible outcomes. To advance an urban circular economy, cities must dismantle these institutional path dependencies. Reform requires multi-sectoral coordination, legal recognition of informal systems, and performance-based partnerships grounded in clear accountability. Without these reforms, circular economy transitions will remain aspirational rather than operational.

5.5 Digital Tools for Urban Circularity

Digital technologies are increasingly enabling cities in the Global South to operationalise circular economy models, particularly in urban waste and water management. Tools (e.g., digital twins, blockchain platforms, and AI) now assist municipal authorities in improving traceability, decision-making, and resource optimisation. However, several persistent barriers (e.g., legal restrictions, interoperability gaps, and data fragmentation) limit their widespread adoption. Effective deployment of these tools requires both robust digital infrastructure and coordinated institutional support.

Digital twin technology has emerged as a powerful tool for sustainable water management. In the Limpopo River Basin, the International Water Management Institute (IWMI) developed a digital twin prototype that enables the real-time visualisation of hydrological dynamics, stakeholder simulation, and impact forecasting (Garcia Andarcia et al., 2024). This system integrates AI-based predictions, land-use models, and climate variables to support decision-making regarding conservation, irrigation, and infrastructure. These capabilities enable local and regional agencies to simulate the outcomes of water policies and investments prior to implementation, thereby enhancing efficiency and environmental sustainability (Garcia Andarcia et al., 2024). Although not fully deployed at the municipal scale, the Limpopo example provides proof of concept for cities seeking to replicate digital twin infrastructure.

AI and IoT technologies have significantly improved solid waste sorting and recovery in several cities in Latin America. Bijos et al. (2022)

documented the application of machine learning algorithms in waste management systems throughout the region. These models classify waste composition data, enhance the use of IoT-enabled smart bins, and integrate with geographic information systems (GIS) to optimise collection routes and separation centres. Although data unreliability and fragmented time series limit model accuracy, AI tools have demonstrated potential to increase recyclable output, lower sorting costs, and reduce methane emissions from landfill-bound waste (Bijos et al., 2022). The integration of informal waste collectors into these systems is an open challenge, although hybrid AI-IoT models offer opportunities to bridge this gap.

Blockchain-based solutions are also playing a growing role in urban circularity, particularly under Extended Producer Responsibility (EPR) schemes. In Southeast Asia, a blockchain platform developed in Singapore and Amsterdam tracks plastic waste along reverse logistics chains, enabling brand owners to meet their 20–30% recycling obligations under national regulations (TechInnovation, 2021). The system provides tamper-proof, auditable trails of material flow and financial contributions, linking investors, non-governmental organisations (NGOs), and recycling operators. This innovation addresses the persistent gap between EPR legislation and actual recycling infrastructure by enabling targeted investments in new waste-processing capacity. However, high dependency on initial donors or corporate backing limits scalability across cities with weaker financial ecosystems.

Digital transformation efforts in Latin America and the Caribbean (LAC) highlight both the promise and the complexity of scaling circular economy tools. According to the Inter-American Development Bank (IDB), the LAC region generated approximately 230.47 million tonnes of municipal solid waste in 2021, with only 4.39% entering recovery systems (IDB, 2024). To address this issue, several cities have deployed business intelligence (BI), fleet-tracking, and customer-management platforms to optimise waste-service delivery and increase recycling rates. AI and cloud computing tools now support data collection and visualisation, enabling local authorities to track circular economy targets. However, limited interoperability between municipal platforms and poor institutional digital maturity often prevent the consolidation of circular datasets across jurisdictions.

Privacy regulations present significant challenges to digital circular economy initiatives. In Brazil, the General Data Protection Law (LGPD) imposes restrictions on the sharing of detailed household data, thereby impeding the training of AI models and the establishment of behavioural feedback loops (IDB, 2024). Additionally, many platforms lack standardised application programming interfaces (APIs), which constrains their capacity to facilitate communication across different cities or regions. As discussed in Chapter 2, these deficiencies in digital infrastructure substantially limit the potential of emerging tools to deliver the integrated benefits of the circular economy.

5.6 Comparative Regional Analysis

Circular economy implementation across the Global South exhibits significant variation in institutional frameworks, technological integration, and community engagement. Comparative regional evidence from Africa, Asia, and Latin America reveals both the promise and fragmentation that shape the circular transitions in food and urban systems.

In Africa, innovative interventions by the private sector have effectively addressed significant deficiencies in food logistics. In Nigeria, the startup Ecotutu has established a solar-powered cold chain infrastructure at Lagos's Mile 12 Market, where post-harvest losses affect up to 45% of perishable produce, valued at approximately $4 billion annually (Okojie, 2023). By offering "pay-as-you-chill" cold storage solutions, Ecotutu has successfully bridged the infrastructure gap for informal traders and aggregators without necessitating upfront investment. However, urban governance has become increasingly fragmented. The broader waste management system in Lagos lacks formal waste segregation and reliable collection, thereby limiting the scalability of the circular economy beyond pilot programs (Oladosu et al., 2024). Governance gaps, unclear mandates, and inadequate infrastructure continue to impede the sustainable expansion of the urban circular economy in the region.

In Asia, Vietnam stands out as a promising frontier for circular economy development. Its One Million Hectares program integrates certified seeds, mechanised planting, site-specific fertiliser use, as well as rice-straw reuse for low-emission rice farming. This initiative has achieved yields of 6.3–6.5 tonnes per hectare, compared with 5.8 tonnes under traditional methods, while reducing greenhouse gas emissions by at least 2 tonnes CO_2 equivalent per hectare (IRRI, 2024). The project's alignment with the circular economy principles demonstrates how national ministries, research institutes, and cooperatives can coordinate their technological and environmental goals. Similarly, Vietnam's rice straw innovations, underpinned by blockchain-enabled traceability and training partnerships, have embedded circular economy strategies into agricultural policy (UNDP, 2024). In contrast, the Philippines illustrates the tension between informal actors in the circular economy and formal urban planning. In Tondo, Manila, waste pickers operate informal materials recovery networks that are deeply embedded in local spatial and economic systems. Yet, the city's planning regime marginalises these actors through zoning regulations and limited recognition, creating a structural conflict between urban governance and circular practices (Sicam, 2023).

Latin America demonstrates both regulatory promise and administrative constraints. In Chía, Colombia, local authorities and stakeholders have piloted resource recovery from organic waste using participatory governance models. While these efforts support innovation and local capacity-building, weak inter-agency coordination and limited environmental data-sharing constrain scalability (Aguilar et al., 2024). More broadly, the region faces a paradox in adopting a circular economy: although Colombia and Brazil have pioneered policies on food waste and urban agriculture, persistent inequality, inadequate monitoring, and informal systems have hindered effective integration. Regional consumption data further highlights systemic contradictions. Meat accounts for less than 13% of Latin American diets yet contributes more than 70% of food-related greenhouse gas emissions, underscoring the urgent need for systemic, circular dietary shifts (Marrero et al., 2022).

Across these regions, a consistent trend emerges: successful implementation of the circular economy depends less on technology alone and more on institutional strength and the inclusiveness of governance. In Africa, entrepreneurial innovation outpaces municipal coordination. In Asia, a circular economy thrives, where national policy aligns with decentralised experimentation. In Latin America, participatory frameworks show potential, but institutional fragmentation weakens their impact. Advancing circular economy transitions will therefore require not only infrastructure and investment but also deliberate reform of regulatory systems and stakeholder networks that currently impede circular integration in the Global South.

5.7 Recommendations and Conclusion

In this chapter, we examined how institutional conditions, technological integration, as well as governance dynamics shape circular economy transitions in food and urban systems across emerging economies. Drawing on comparative case studies, we propose actionable pathways for policy, business, and capacity-building.

Policy: Governments should harmonise regional circular economy frameworks, particularly in food waste regulation and digital infrastructure, across blocs such as ASEAN and the African Union. National and municipal authorities must also introduce circular economy performance benchmarks to enable cities and sectors to systematically track material recovery, emissions reduction, and reuse rates.

Business: The private sector should scale modular circular economy technologies (e.g., blockchain for food traceability, IoT kits for cold storage) that function in low-infrastructure environments. Evidence from Vietnam's rice value chain and Lagos's market-led cold chain initiatives shows that adaptable solutions can enhance both productivity and environmental performance. National governments should promote business incubation schemes tailored to urban circular economy startups, especially those that integrate informal sector actors.

Research & Capacity-Building: Policymakers and development partners must invest in localised circular economy pilot programs and community-driven experimentation. Training curricula should target urban planners, agricultural extension workers, and agri-tech developers, with emphasis on circular economy metrics, data interoperability, as well as inclusive design strategies. Participatory models and informal networks (e.g., waste pickers in Manila, decentralised market systems in Lagos) often drive implementation but require institutional recognition and technical support to scale.

References

Africa Regenerative Agriculture Study Group. (2021). *Regenerative agriculture: An opportunity for businesses and society to restore degraded land in Africa*. IUCN. https://iucn.org/sites/default/files/2022-06/regnererative_agriculture_in_africa_report_2021_compressed.pdf

AGRA. (2021). *Africa agriculture status report: A decade of action—Building sustainable and resilient food systems in Africa*. Alliance for a Green Revolution in Africa. https://afs-forum.org/wp-content/uploads/2021/09/AASR-2021-A-Decade-of-Action-_Building-Sustainable-and-Resilient-Food-Systems-in-Africa-1.pdf

Aguilar-Hernandez, G. A., Van Hoof, B., Conde, Á., Kahhat, R., & Pabón-Pereira, C. (2024). Enabling mechanisms for circularity in Latin America and the Caribbean. *Journal of Circular Economy, 2*(3). https://doi.org/10.55845/IKH17118

Albaladejo, M., Amann, J., Cantore, N., Flammini, A., Marin, G., & Mazzanti, M. (2023). *Assessing the socio-economic impact of the circular economy through input-output modelling: Evidence from developing countries*. Available at SSRN 5131165.

Amin, S., Khandaker, M. K., Jannat, J., Khan, F., & Rahman, S. Z. (2023). Cooperative environmental governance in urban South Asia: Implications for municipal waste management and waste-to-energy. *Environmental Science and Pollution Research, 30*, 69550–69563. https://doi.org/10.1007/s11356-023-27152-5

Bijos, J. C. B. F., Zanta, V. M., Morató, J., Queiroz, L. M., & Oliveira-Esquerre, K. P. S. R. (2022). Improving circularity in municipal solid waste management through machine learning in Latin America and the Caribbean. *Sustainable Chemistry and Pharmacy, 28*, 100740. https://doi.org/10.1016/j.scp.2022.100740

Bloomberg (2025). Circular City Barometer. https://sponsored.bloomberg.com/immersive/holcim/circular-cities/barometer

Calì, M., Cantore, N., Marin, G., Mazzanti, M., Nicolli, F., & Presidente, G. (2023). Energy prices and the economic performance of firms in emerging countries. *Structural Change and Economic Dynamics, 66*, 357–366.

Challa, L. N. (2025). Constraints faced by farm women in accessing and utilisation of digital extension services. *Gujarat Journal of Extension Education, 38*(1), 154–162.

Garcia Andarcia, M., Dickens, C., Silva, P., Matheswaran, K., & Koo, J. (2024). *Digital Twin for management of water resources in the Limpopo River Basin: A concept*. International Water Management Institute (IWMI). https://cgspace.cgiar.org/server/api/core/bitstreams/f3fd37c9-bb7f-4503-bffd-5a4a1bf26383/content

IDB. (2024, September). *Digital transformation of solid waste management: Waste collection innovation, business intelligence, and digital technologies to transition waste management towards circularity in Latin America and the Caribbean* (Technical Note No. IDB-TN-0301). Inter-American Development Bank. https://publications.iadb.org/en/publications/english/viewer/technical-note-no-idb-tn-0301-vf.pdf

IRRI. (2024, July 23). *Vietnam's pilot low-emission rice farming shows promise: Increased yields, profits and sustainability*. International Rice Research Institute. https://www.cgiar.org/news-events/news/vietnams-pilot-low-emission-rice-farming-shows-promise-increased-yields-profits-and-sustainability/

Kabiri, S. (2024). *A basket of regenerative agriculture technologies for the improvement of soil health in Africa: 50 technologies for on-farm demonstrations*. Sasakawa Africa Association. https://www.saa-safe.org/elfiles/xc85X4Fu/Size%20adjusted_FIN%20-%20web%20compressed%20-%20Basket%20of%20RA%20Tech%202024.pdf

Marrero, A., Anderson, E., de la Vega, C., Beltran, V., Haneuse, S., Golden, C., & Mattei, J. (2022). An integrated assessment of environmental sustainability and nutrient availability of food consumption patterns in Latin America and the Caribbean. *The American Journal of Clinical Nutrition, 116*(5), 1265–1277. https://doi.org/10.1093/ajcn/nqac220

Nutrition Connect. (2023). *Food Safety and Standards Authority of India (FSSAI): Guiding optimisation of surplus food donation*. https://nutritionconnect.org/food-safety-standards-authority-india-fssai-guiding-optimisation-surplus-food-donation

Okojie, J. (2023, March 29). *Ecotutu to launch cold chain infrastructure to tackle post-harvest losses*. BusinessDay. https://businessday.ng/agriculture/article/ecotutu-to-launch-cold-chain-infrastructure-to-tackle-post-harvest-losses/

Oladosu, O., Abiodun, O. A., Oloruntoba, E. O., & Adegoroye, A. (2024). *Evaluating urban service delivery in Lagos State Nigeria: A bid to enhance sustainable waste management*. ResearchGate. https://www.researchgate.net/publication/378526141

Schindler, M., & Dionisio, R. (2021). A framework to assess impacts of path dependence on urban planning outcomes, induced through the use of decision-support tools. *Cities, 115*, 103256. https://doi.org/10.1016/j.cities.2021.103256

Sicam, O. (2023). The production of space in the informal waste economy: Waste picking in the Tondo Manila Bay Area. *The Journal of Public Space, 8*(1), 43–68. https://doi.org/10.32891/jps.v8i1.1212

TechInnovation. (2021). *A platform to commercially scale plastic recycling*. https://na.eventscloud.com/website/30321/a-platform-to-commercially-scale-plastic-recycling/

UNDP. (2024, July 19). *Training programme on circular economy & rice straw innovations in the rice value chain*. United Nations Development Programme Vietnam. https://www.undp.org/vietnam/press-releases/training-program-circular-economy-rice-straw-innovations-rice-value-chain

UNFCCC. (2024). *Use of agro-weather tool for enhancing early warning and adaptation for farmers—Kenya*. United Nations Framework Convention on Climate Change. https://unfccc.int/climate-action/momentum-for-change/activity-database/use-of-agro-weather-tool-for-enhancing-early-warning-and-adaptation-for-farmersdatabase/use-of-agro-weather-tool-for-enhancing-early-warning-and-adaptation-for-farmers

World Bank. (2023). *5 trends in public-private partnerships in water supply and sanitation*. https://ppp.worldbank.org/public-private-partnership/5-trends-public-private-partnerships-water-supply-and-sanitation

PART III

Policy, Governance, and Future Directions

CHAPTER 6

Policy, Regulation, and Global Implications for Circularity and Net-Zero

Abstract In this chapter, we examine how policies and regulatory frameworks facilitate circular economy adoption and net-zero transitions in emerging markets. With a focus on Sub-Saharan Africa, Southeast Asia, and Latin America, we apply Institutional Theory to analyse identifiable governance barriers (e.g., regulatory fragmentation, informal sector dominance). Our analysis highlights the necessity of adaptive, multi-level, and inclusive governance models that integrate informal actors and strengthen institutional legitimacy. We argue that a practical policy roadmap will mainstream national incentives, regional standard harmonisation, and strategic international engagement. Our findings offer critical insights for policymakers seeking to operationalise circular economy and net-zero transitions in complex institutional environments in developing economies.

Keywords Circular economy · Net-Zero transition · Policy frameworks · Regulation · Emerging markets · Governance barriers · Renewable energy targets · Institutional theory

O. Evans and O. Adeola, *Innovations in Circular Economy and Net Zero*, https://doi.org/10.1007/978-3-032-22094-3_6

6.1 Introduction

Policies and regulations can serve as critical catalysts for accelerating circular economy adoption and net-zero transitions, particularly in emerging markets where institutional and infrastructural gaps persist (Ruth & El-Amin, 2025; Rweyendela & Kombe, 2021). Regulatory frameworks establish essential conditions for emissions monitoring, waste management, and resource efficiency. However, in many low- and middle-income countries, these frameworks are often fragmented, weakly enforced, or disconnected from prevailing informal sector activities that deliver essential circular economy functions (Rasheed et al., 2024). Table 6.1 outlines the adoption rates and impacts of four different policy mechanisms in 2024: Renewable Energy Targets, Auctions/Tenders, Net Metering, and Feed-in Tariffs, based on data from BloombergNEF's *Climatescope* Survey of 110 emerging markets.

Diversity of motivations and outcomes characterises the policy landscapes of Sub-Saharan Africa, Southeast Asia, and Latin America. Sub-Saharan African economies frequently rely on informal systems due to regulatory voids and under-resourced enforcement agencies (Ruth & El-Amin, 2025).

Table 6.1 Policy frameworks

Policy type	***Share of Emerging Markets with Policy Mechanisms in force*** *(2024)*	*Impact*
Renewable Energy Targets	95%	Often lack implementation mechanisms
Auctions/Tenders	64%	Key mechanism for attracting investment and improving market competitiveness
Net Metering	63%	Supports distributed solar growth
Feed-in Tariffs	34%	Increasingly being replaced by auctions/ tenders

Data source BloombergNEF (2024)

Institutional Theory offers a valuable analytical lens for understanding the diverse governance contexts in emerging economies. It highlights how formal regulatory voids and informal sector dominance can undermine the enforcement of circular economy policy, and how coercive, mimetic, and normative pressures shape institutional evolution (Dragomir et al., 2023). Applying this theoretical framework enables the identification of entrenched governance barriers and institutional weaknesses that limit sustainable transitions in emerging markets. In this chapter, we critically examine how policy and governance interventions can enable circular economy and net-zero transitions in emerging markets. We evaluate regulatory frameworks, identify institutional constraints, and propose actionable multi-level policy paths that incorporate both formal and informal practices. By advancing understanding of how policies function as enablers (and where institutional shortcomings persist), this analysis contributes to shaping inclusive, context-sensitive strategies for sustainable development in the Global South.

6.2 Policy Landscapes and Governance Barriers in Emerging Markets

In Africa, Asia, and Latin America, emerging economies (e.g., South Africa, Indonesia, Brazil) demonstrate contrasting yet instructive policy landscapes for circular economy and net-zero transitions. Each case reveals that formal commitments often coexist with structural governance deficiencies. In Sub-Saharan Africa, South Africa's policy environment reveals both ambition and fragmentation. The country's Low Emission Development Strategy (LEDS), adopted in 2020, formally commits South Africa to the achievement of net-zero emissions by 2050 (Chapungu et al., 2022). Complementary frameworks (e.g., the National Waste Management Strategy, the Carbon Tax Act of 2019) target emissions reductions and waste management improvements. However, these instruments operate in silos, indicative of the interdepartmental fragmentation of national, provincial and municipal authorities, and diminished regulatory coherence (Mugisha, 2025). Only 64% of local governments report compliance with national waste regulations, which indicates limited enforcement capacity (Mugisha, 2025). Informal waste pickers dominate recycling activities, recovering approximately 80% of post-consumer packaging waste nationwide (Reis-Filho et al., 2025). Institutional voids explain this dynamic: when formal regulations exist but are not effectively enforced, informal systems substitute as default governance mechanisms (Mugisha, 2025).

In Southeast Asia, Indonesia exhibits policy ambition, but it is undermined by entrenched structural deficiencies. The country's 2024 National Electricity Plan allocates 60% of electricity generation to coal, despite official targets of 75 GW of renewable energy capacity by 2040 (International Energy Agency [IEA], 2022). Yet, in 2025, Indonesia signed a US$10 billion agreement with Singapore to establish a green industrial zone for solar panel and battery production (Net Zero Policy Lab [NZPL], 2025). Fragmented regulatory responsibilities between national ministries exacerbate administrative inefficiencies (Indonesia Business Post, 2025). Moreover, Indonesia underinvests in research, development, and technical education, which constrains the country's capacity to operationalise circular economy strategies (NZPL, 2025). In waste management, the informal sector handles approximately 70% of recyclable material collection in urban areas. However, national frameworks exclude these actors from formal circular economy strategies, indicating a governance gap rather than a policy choice (Reis-Filho et al., 2025). Indonesia's institutional void manifests through parallel formal commitments and reliance on informal practices.

In Latin America, Brazil reflects regulatory decentralisation despite regional leadership in renewable energy. The 2010 National Solid Waste Policy mandates extended producer responsibility (EPR) and municipal recycling, yet only 54% of municipalities implemented recycling programs by 2024 (Gallego-Schmid et al., 2024). Regulatory enforcement varies across states, driven by conflicting subnational priorities and weak federal oversight (Organisation for Economic Co-operation and Development [OECD], 2025). Brazil's climate action framework primarily relies on non-market-based instruments, accounting for 43% of interventions in 2023, while carbon pricing remains marginal (OECD, 2025). Institutional Theory identifies entrenched industrial interests as inhibitors of reform, promoting institutional voids where regulations exist without operational capacity (Gallego-Schmid et al., 2024). Informal waste pickers manage over 90% of Brazil's recyclable waste (Reis-Filho et al., 2025); however, policy frameworks classify these workers as peripheral actors.

Across Africa, Asia, and Latin America, informal economies play a critical role in circular economy functions, particularly in waste collection and resource recovery. Rather than representing policy failure, these informal systems reflect hybrid institutional arrangements, wherein informal practices compensate for weak formal mechanisms (Reis-Filho et al., 2025). However, persistent exclusion from national frameworks marginalises their roles and limits their potential scalability. Institutional Theory conceptualises these systems as hybrid institutional fields: informal structures operate parallel to formal institutions, but without integration or state support.

Policy commitment to circularity exhibits significant variation across emerging markets, reflecting differences in political will, institutional capacity, and regulatory maturity (see Fig. 6.1). Bogotá stands out with a perfect score of 100, highlighting the efficacy of Colombia's national circular economy strategy and the city's implementation of comprehensive roadmaps addressing emissions, sustainable infrastructure, and equitable development. Mexico City follows with a moderate score of 50, indicating a fragmented yet developing regulatory framework. Buenos Aires and Lagos both receive a middling score of 33, suggesting sporadic policy instrument usage or limited institutional coordination. In contrast, Dubai and Quezon City register a low score of 17, despite their participation in various circular initiatives, suggesting a delay in formalising these into roadmaps. Johannesburg and Nairobi report an absence of formal circularity-aligned policy roadmaps, underscoring institutional inertia or competing development priorities. These disparities underscore the uneven policy frameworks supporting urban transitions and the critical need for globally coordinated regulatory ambition, particularly in rapidly urbanising regions.

6.3 Unlocking National-Level Policy Opportunities

Emerging markets must adopt coordinated and context-sensitive policies to advance the circular economy and net-zero objectives. Four national-level interventions provide critical opportunities: fiscal incentives for sustainable production and consumption, mandatory standards for recycling and product design, formal integration of informal waste sector workers, and selective investment in digital infrastructure. However, these interventions must respond to regional variations in industrial capacity, institutional structures, and resource constraints.

Fiscal policy remains underutilised as a tool for promoting circular economy transitions in emerging economies. South Africa is a notable exception, with its Carbon Tax Act of 2019, which introduced Africa's

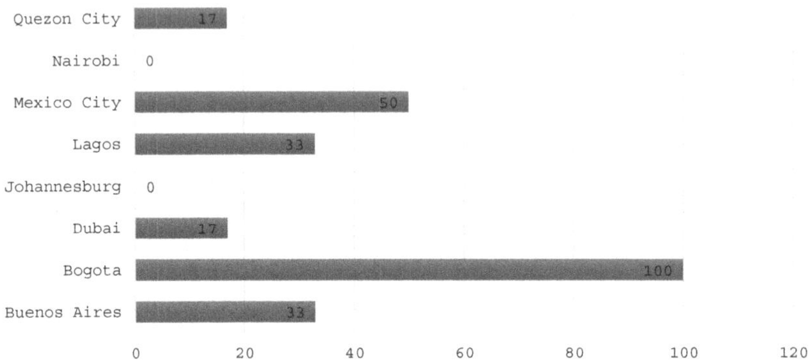

Fig. 6.1 National-Level Policy and Roadmap Scores Across Selected Cities (*Source* Bloomberg [2025])

first national carbon pricing instrument. Although the tax is diluted by allowances that enable emitters to offset up to 95% of their liabilities, it nonetheless anchors South Africa's fiscal framework for a low-carbon transition (Baker, 2022; International Monetary Fund [IMF], 2023). The expansion of fiscal incentives beyond carbon pricing is now essential. Tax credits for recycled-content products, grants for eco-innovation initiatives, and green VAT exemptions could support sustainable production and consumption patterns. In contrast, Indonesia's fiscal support is largely concentrated in its green industrialisation program. The government's biofuel mandates and subsidies for electric-vehicle battery production reflect a resource-based industrial strategy that prioritises downstream value-chain development but neglects resource circularity (Net Zero Policy Lab [NZPL], 2025). To ensure long-term resource efficiency, Indonesia must embed circular economy requirements directly into these fiscal instruments. Similarly, Brazil emphasises fiscal instruments in its renewable energy sector but provides limited support for circular economy innovations, highlighting a gap between climate policy and waste management.

Mandatory standards (e.g., recycling quotas, eco-design regulations) provide direct regulatory leverage for circular economy transitions. Brazil's National Solid Waste Policy mandates extended producer responsibility (EPR) for producers and importers but covers only 54% of municipalities due to fragmented regulatory oversight and limited federal enforcement capacity (Gallego-Schmid et al., 2025). Scaling the circular economy in Brazil requires national minimum recycling standards, enforceable EPR obligations, as well as product-specific eco-design requirements targeting reparability, recyclability, and post-consumer waste reduction. Indonesia's localisation strategy, centred on manufacturing expansion, presents a clear policy window for integrating mandatory circular economy regulations into industrial policy (International Energy Agency [IEA], 2022). By mandating eco-design standards for locally manufactured products, Indonesia can institutionalise circularity within its growing industrial base.

The informal waste sector is a structural pillar of circular economy practices across Sub-Saharan Africa and Southeast Asia. In South Africa, informal waste pickers recover between 80 and 90% of post-consumer plastic packaging, diverting materials from landfill and generating over R750 million in landfill cost savings annually (ESG Education, n.d.). Despite these contributions, waste pickers operate without legal recognition, employment protections, or formal access to municipal waste contracts. Most workers earn between R50 and R200 per day under hazardous conditions, often without access to health insurance or safety equipment (ESG Education, n.d.). Formalising waste pickers through national registries, health protections, and cooperative models would elevate their role within the formal circular economy. Similarly, in Indonesia, informal waste workers manage approximately 70% of recyclable material, yet they are excluded from policy frameworks (Reis-Filho et al., 2025). Policymakers must institutionalise the contributions of the informal sector through targeted regulations that recognise these workers as essential service providers.

Digital infrastructure investments present a valuable national-level opportunity, but must remain supplemental to foundational waste management infrastructure. Indonesia's digital leadership supports the adoption of blockchain-enabled EPR platforms and traceability systems for recycled materials (NZPL, 2025). However, Southeast Asia's current innovation ecosystem contributes to rising emissions due to the growth of energy-intensive manufacturing (Hardi et al., 2025). National governments must therefore prioritise digital investments that enhance material tracking, implement payment systems for waste pickers, and facilitate regulatory monitoring, while avoiding indiscriminate digitisation that could overwhelm resource-constrained contexts. In Sub-Saharan Africa, digital solutions must complement physical infrastructure investments.

Nigeria's Wecyclers and South Africa's Regenize demonstrate that mobile reward systems and digital payments can incentivise waste collection and integrate informal workers into formal value chains (Henriksen, 2021). Scaling these models across the continent will require embedding digital components within broader waste management reforms.

South Africa's experience with the Carbon Tax Act and waste picker formalisation highlights the potential of combined fiscal and social policy interventions to drive inclusive circular economy transitions. Although the carbon tax has yet to yield significant emissions reductions due to exemptions, it positions South Africa as a continental leader in carbon pricing (Baker, 2022). Simultaneously, the integration of waste pickers into municipal systems transforms previously informal workers into recognised economic agents, thereby elevating recycling rates and promoting socio-economic inclusion (Henriksen, 2021). This dual approach (linking fiscal reform with informal sector formalisation) demonstrates a pragmatic, scalable policy framework for national circular economy advancement.

6.4 Regional Cooperation and Standard Harmonisation

Regional cooperation is a critical enabler of circular economy and net-zero transitions in emerging markets. Regional frameworks enhance regulatory consistency, facilitate knowledge sharing, and support capacity-building across states with varying levels of institutional readiness. However, existing mechanisms often function as advisory platforms rather than enforceable regimes, underscoring the need for coordinated institutional development.

In Southeast Asia, the ASEAN Circular Economy Strategic Framework, adopted in 2021, outlines five shared strategic priorities, including harmonised standards, sustainable production models, and digital technology applications (ASEAN Secretariat, 2021). While the framework functions as a policy blueprint rather than a binding agreement, it promotes convergence in national circular economy approaches. The ASEAN Circularity Coalition, launched in 2024, strengthens this regional collaboration by establishing platforms for joint projects and policy dialogues (EU-ASEAN Business Council, 2024). However, ASEAN lacks centralised enforcement mechanisms to ensure uniform implementation, which limits the framework's operational influence. Private sector platforms (e.g., Sembcorp's GoNetZero™, CHINT's Digital Carbon

Management Platform) illustrate regionally relevant digital monitoring solutions (CHINT, 2024; Sembcorp, 2025). Nevertheless, these are proprietary tools adopted by individual firms and are distinct from the ASEAN-led initiatives. Policymakers could consider the adaptation of such models within a coordinated ASEAN digital reporting infrastructure, yet no such integration currently exists.

In Africa, the African Green Stimulus Programme (AGSP), endorsed by the African Union in 2022, emphasises a continent-wide green recovery through partnerships, technical cooperation, as well as capacity-building (African Union, 2022). AGSP's broad agenda includes circular economy and net-zero elements, but prioritises adaptation and economic recovery. Africa's structural finance deficits impede regional infrastructure development; between 2016 and 2019, African countries received less than US$20 billion, compared with the US$3 trillion required to implement their Nationally Determined Contributions (NDCs) (Murombedzi & Munang, 2023). Voluntary carbon markets are under-developed, despite significant sequestration potential (Murombedzi & Munang, 2023). While harmonised carbon certification frameworks could theoretically mobilise climate finance, the continent's institutional fragmentation currently precludes rapid consolidation. Regional cooperation should thus focus on the development of interoperable data-sharing protocols and regional capacity-building hubs to strengthen carbon accounting capabilities.

In Latin America, MERCOSUR has intensified environmental coordination, particularly through the Environment Working Subgroup (SGT-6). In 2021, MERCOSUR countries launched a joint negotiation platform on climate change policy (MERCOSUR, 2021). Although the bloc lacks binding environmental standards, it has progressively incorporated Sustainable Development Goals (SDGs) into its policy frameworks, with Brazil playing a central role (da Silva & Bermejo, 2023). Public–private partnerships (PPPs), especially in water and sanitation, demonstrate MERCOSUR's capacity to coordinate infrastructure development (Inter-American Development Bank, 2021). The expansion of such PPP frameworks to waste management and circular economy infrastructure represents a pragmatic pathway for regional cooperation.

Across these regions, the proliferation of voluntary carbon certification standards intensifies the need for harmonisation. Global carbon markets witnessed 15 new certification schemes emerge in 2023 alone, contributing to increased market fragmentation (Hamerkop, 2025).

While global standard consolidation is elusive, regional harmonisation could simplify compliance and reduce costs for exporters. Defining harmonised standards, however, requires specificity. Policymakers should prioritise standardisation in two domains: (1) carbon accounting and reporting protocols, aligned with ISO 14064-1:2018 and the Greenhouse Gas (GHG) Protocol; and (2) circular economy product standards, including recyclability criteria and labelling regulations.

Therefore, the establishment of regional capacity-building platforms could address institutional voids, particularly in technical competencies related to emissions reporting and resource monitoring. Shared digital infrastructure (e.g., interoperable emissions databases, regional certification registries) may offer longer-term opportunities. However, sovereignty concerns and resource disparities necessitate an incremental and consultative approach to shared infrastructure development. Thus, while regional frameworks exist across ASEAN, Africa, and MERCOSUR, their effectiveness depends on the translation of strategic coordination into operational standardisation and enforceable mechanisms (see Table 6.2).

6.5 International Mechanisms and Trade Implications

International trade governance increasingly shapes the trajectory of circular economy adoption and net-zero transitions in emerging markets. Key mechanisms (e.g., the Carbon Border Adjustment Mechanism [CBAM], WTO negotiations on environmental goods and services, OECD regulatory frameworks, the Paris Agreement) exert substantial influence over export competitiveness and regulatory compliance requirements.

The European Union's CBAM is a critical development for carbon leakage prevention strategies. Enacted through Regulation (EU) 2023/956, CBAM imposes an embedded carbon cost on imports of selected products, initially covering cement, aluminium, steel, fertilisers, electricity, and hydrogen (European Union, 2023). Commencing 2026, identifiable financial obligations will apply, calibrated against the EU Emissions Trading System (European Commission, 2024). Emerging market exporters face significant risks under CBAM, particularly in energy-intensive sectors. Wang (2025) identifies steel, cement, aluminium, and chemicals as the most vulnerable sectors to competitive erosion due to

Table 6.2 Comparative analysis of regional cooperation for Circular Economy (CE)/Net Zero (NZ) in emerging markets

Criteria	*ASEAN*	*Africa (African Union)*	*MERCOSUR*
Core Framework	ASEAN Circular Economy Strategic Framework (2021); ASEAN Circularity Coalition (2024)	African Green Stimulus Programme (AGSP, 2022)	MERCOSUR Environmental Agenda (SGT-6), 2021 climate platform
Framework Nature	Strategic coordination (non-binding)	Strategic recovery initiative (advisory)	Policy dialogue platform (advisory, limited enforcement)
Policy Focus	CE product standards; digital monitoring; sustainable production models	Green recovery; circular economy inclusion; regional adaptation cooperation	SDG integration; climate policy negotiations; waste management
Institutional Maturity	High (coordinated digital initiatives in private sector; policy alignment structures in place)	Moderate (continental frameworks with fragmented national adoption)	Low–Moderate (gradual SDG adoption, policy alignment nascent)
Operational Mechanisms	Joint projects; knowledge-sharing platforms; informal digital convergence	Capacity-building partnerships; cross-border cooperation initiatives	Public–private partnerships in water/waste sectors
Standard Harmonisation Level	Emerging; no binding CE/NZ product or reporting standards	Fragmented; absence of carbon certification standardisation	Weak; no binding regional environmental or circular economy standards
Digital Infrastructure Role	High potential; private sector platforms (GoNetZero™, CHINT) as models	Minimal; focus on capacity-building over digital integration	Limited; digital monitoring not prioritised

(continued)

Table 6.2 (continued)

Criteria	*ASEAN*	*Africa (African Union)*	*MERCOSUR*
Shared Infrastructure	Not yet developed; potential for ASEAN-level digital registries	Not feasible short term; potential in interoperable data-sharing	Not pursued; PPP models dominate waste infrastructure strategy
Key Limitation	Lack of enforceable mechanisms	Severe financial and institutional capacity gaps	Fragmented governance; policy asymmetry across members
Strategic Recommendation	Formalize digital monitoring within ASEAN framework; develop product standards	Establish regional certification standards; focus on capacity-building hubs	Focus on infrastructure PPPs and gradual standard convergence

their high embodied emissions and limited decarbonisation. For emerging economies that rely heavily on coal-based energy, the CBAM poses a direct threat to exports.

Indonesia illustrates these vulnerabilities. The country's steel industry, central to its industrialisation agenda, depends on carbon-intensive electricity and metallurgical processes (Indonesia Business Post, 2025). The EU market, which accounted for €210 billion in steel imports in 2023, now presents substantial trade barriers unless Indonesian producers can validate emissions reductions or purchase CBAM certificates (European Commission, 2024). While Indonesia's National Electricity Plan commits to 75 GW of renewable energy capacity by 2040, the current electricity generation is 60% coal-based, which constrains decarbonisation in the short term (Indonesia Business Post, 2025). Nevertheless, CBAM compliance also has strategic opportunities. Indonesian exporters who are able to implement verifiable emissions accounting systems and invest in production efficiency may preserve market access and gain a competitive advantage over their non-compliant regional peers.

In parallel, the Paris Agreement imposes regulatory pressures through NDC revision cycles. The United Nations Framework Convention on Climate Change (UNFCCC, 2025) underscores that emerging economies must progressively strengthen their mitigation commitments to align with the 1.5 °C target. However, resource constraints hinder their effective implementation. For example, African countries required an estimated US$3 trillion for NDC execution but secured only US$20 billion between 2016 and 2019 (Murombedzi & Munang, 2023). Similar financing and institutional capacity deficits afflict Southeast Asian economies, which limit their ability to align industrial exports with low-carbon benchmarks.

At the multilateral level, World Trade Organization (WTO) negotiations on environmental goods and services (EGS) liberalisation offer limited immediate relief. While liberalisation theoretically facilitates the adoption of the circular economy by reducing tariffs on recycling technologies and secondary raw materials, definitional disputes and regulatory divergence have stalled meaningful progress (Sende, 2023). Barrie et al. (2022) highlight that existing trade classifications inadequately reflect circular goods, creating procedural complexities that disadvantage emerging markets. Moreover, poorly regulated circular trade risks facilitating illicit waste flows, underscoring the need for harmonised definitions and robust enforcement frameworks.

OECD regulatory frameworks indirectly shape supply chain decarbonisation expectations. Although originally designed for conflict minerals, the OECD's *Due Diligence Guidance for Responsible Supply Chains* has fuelled broader transparency expectations among buyers in OECD markets (OECD, 2016). While this guidance does not mandate carbon reporting, its widespread adoption creates de facto compliance pressures, requiring exporters from emerging markets to demonstrate mitigation of environmental and social risks. In nickel and mineral supply chains, these frameworks increasingly intersect with climate standards, influencing buyers' decisions and market access conditions.

To address these converging pressures, emerging markets must adopt multipronged strategies. The use of WTO forums to advocate for simplified trade classifications and capacity-building support is a medium-term goal that acknowledges the current stagnation in negotiations. Concurrently, expanding access to voluntary carbon markets and climate-linked investment instruments can facilitate emissions reductions in key export sectors (Murombedzi & Munang, 2023). Critically, domestic institutional strengthening is the most immediate priority. Investments in emissions monitoring infrastructure, verifiable reporting protocols, and production decarbonisation must precede effective engagement with CBAM and OECD-aligned supply chain requirements.

6.6 Carbon Pricing and the EU CBAM: Implications for Developing Countries

The European Union's Carbon Border Adjustment Mechanism (CBAM) establishes a pivotal link between climate regulation and global trade. Operating alongside the EU Emissions Trading System (ETS), CBAM imposes a carbon price on selected imports (e.g., aluminium, iron and steel, cement, fertilisers, electricity, and hydrogen) to prevent carbon leakage and preserve the competitiveness of EU industries subject to domestic climate constraints (Maliszewska et al., 2025). For developing countries, CBAM presents both systemic risks and strategic opportunities, depending on each country's emissions intensity and its reliance on EU markets for exports.

Developing countries must first evaluate their exposure to CBAM using sector-specific carbon-cost metrics. The World Bank's CBAM Exposure Index, which measures excess carbon payments as a share of a sector's global export value, identifies Mozambique as the most exposed country (see Fig. 6.2). Its aluminium sector, responsible for 97% of aluminium exports to the EU, emits 0.8 kilograms of CO_2 per USD of exports, 7.4 times the EU average. Consequently, excess carbon payments equate to 6% of Mozambique's global aluminium export value (Maliszewska et al., 2025). This level of exposure jeopardises the market share and profitability. Conversely, Ghana, Uzbekistan, and Jordan emit less than the EU average, with exposure values between –0.1% and –0.3%, and therefore may gain a competitive advantage.

Macroeconomic exposure to the Carbon Border Adjustment Mechanism (CBAM), quantified as total excess carbon payments relative to GDP, further underscores existing vulnerabilities (Fig. 6.3). Mozambique once again exhibited the highest exposure at 0.6% of GDP, followed by Ukraine at 0.5% and Egypt at 0.2% (Maliszewska et al., 2025). Although these figures may appear modest, they indicate substantial risk for fiscally constrained economies that depend on exports and are subject to CBAM. Africa, in particular, is anticipated to experience significant sectoral and macroeconomic impacts. Estimates from the London School of Economics and the African Climate Foundation suggest that CBAM could lead to a reduction in African aluminium exports to the EU by 13.9%, iron and steel by 8.2%, and fertilisers by 3.9%. While partial trade diversification into alternative markets, such as China and India, may mitigate some effects, GDP losses across the continent remain likely. A

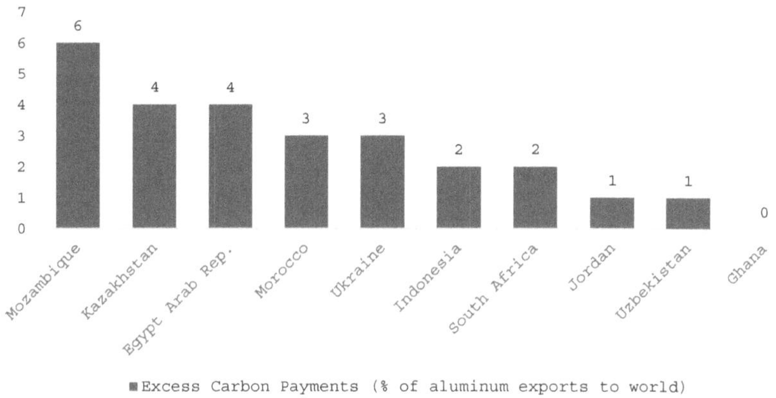

Fig. 6.2 The seven most exposed and the three least exposed countries to the CBAM in the aluminium sector (*Data Source* Maliszewska et al. [2025]. The countries included have export values for all CBAM products to the EU exceeding USD 1 million)

prior analysis projected a 1.6% decline in GDP for Mozambique; however, more recent modelling anticipates a smaller impact due to diversification (Pleeck & Mitchell, 2023).

Despite the significance of the CBAM, carbon pricing uptake among developing countries remains extremely limited. As of 2023, only one

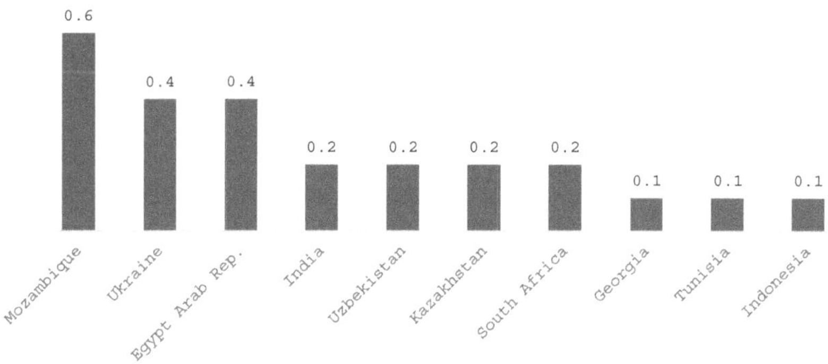

Fig. 6.3 Economic exposure (% of GDP) (*Data source* Maliszewska et al. [2025])

lower-middle-income country (Ukraine) had implemented a carbon price, and just six others had mechanisms planned or under consideration. South Africa's carbon tax remains low in effective value at USD 0.40 per tonne, compared to the EU's market rate of €74–100 (USD 86–116) (Maliszewska et al., 2025). These disparities highlight the competitive disadvantage that exporters face under CBAM.

Policy responses vary in scope and ambition. Byiers and Medinilla (2024) propose four strategies: decarbonise, emulate, challenge, and avoid. "Decarbonise" urges compliance through emissions monitoring and green investments. "Emulate" encourages domestic carbon pricing to recapture CBAM-equivalent revenue. India's proposed export tax on CBAM-related goods reflects this approach, although its WTO compatibility is uncertain due to potential breaches of non-discrimination rules (Pleeck & Mitchell, 2023).

Political tensions have intensified over CBAM's exclusion of least developed countries from exemptions and access to revenues. The European Commission projects annual CBAM revenues of €9.1 billion by 2030, yet all proceeds are earmarked for EU priorities, including repayment of pandemic recovery borrowing (Pleeck & Mitchell, 2023). Developing countries have responded with diplomatic appeals for equitable revenue redistribution, framing CBAM within broader debates over climate justice and differentiated responsibilities. To avoid exclusion from low-carbon global value chains, developing countries must accelerate emissions tracking, assess sectoral carbon exposure, and design feasible domestic pricing schemes. Without decisive action, they risk incurring economic penalties while lacking the institutional means to adapt.

6.7 Institutional Theory Reflection: Rethinking Governance Models

Institutional Theory offers valuable insights into why governance weaknesses persist in a circular economy and in the deployment of net-zero policy in emerging economies. Weak formal regulatory structures often coexist with resilient informal systems that manage resource recovery and waste management in practice (Rweyendela & Kombe, 2021). In Tanzania, Rweyendela and Kombe (2021) found that fragmented legislation and poorly enforced regulations impede circular economy governance, whereas informal sector actors compensate for state deficiencies through community-level recycling and reuse activities. These institutional voids reflect not an absence of governance, but a reliance on alternative, non-state mechanisms shaped by necessity.

Informal institutions and community practices frequently sustain critical circular economy functions when formal enforcement is limited. Ruth and El-Amin (2025) observed that in Sub-Saharan African urban centres, informal waste collectors dominate recycling activities, although precise recovery rates vary and are often undocumented. Similarly, Rasheed et al. (2024) highlighted that South Asian industries rely on informal networks and social norms to facilitate waste recovery and secondary material flows, with minimal formal oversight. While such informal structures contribute to circular economy outcomes, they operate outside legal frameworks and remain largely excluded from national sustainability strategies. Institutional Theory underscores that coercive, normative, and mimetic pressures [which drive corporate climate actions in advanced economies (Dragomir et al., 2023)] exert limited influence in emerging market regulatory environments. Regulatory agencies in Sub-Saharan Africa and South Asia often lack the institutional legitimacy or technical capacities to consistently enforce circular economy regulations (Ruth & El-Amin, 2025; Rweyendela & Kombe, 2021). Consequently, governance frameworks that import rigid regulatory models from industrialised economies frequently underperform in these contexts.

Adaptive hybrid governance models are a pragmatic alternative. Sovacool et al. (2023) noted that countries such as Bhutan and Gabon achieved net-zero progress through decentralised, participatory governance mechanisms that incorporated local practices into national policy frameworks. Recognition of the legitimacy of informal actors, while incrementally extending formal oversight, can bridge governance gaps. Owojori and Anwana (2025) further argue that BRICS economies require institutional coordination and private sector participation to address fossil-fuel dependencies and to implement effective climate governance.

Institutional strengthening must prioritise both capacity development and regulatory legitimacy. Rasheed et al. (2024) recommended targeted regulator training for regulators to improve monitoring and compliance enforcement; however, such interventions should acknowledge structural constraints (e.g., limited resources, bureaucratic fragmentation). UNECA and UNEP (n.d.) have highlighted that African nations often possess under-resourced environmental ministries, contributing to persistent deficits in reporting and enforcement. Without sustained financial and technical support, capacity-building initiatives risk remaining superficial.

Private sector compliance leadership can complement weak public oversight. Dragomir et al. (2023) demonstrate that corporate actors in the EU respond to normative pressure from investors and consumers by adopting carbon reduction targets. Although such pressures are weaker in emerging markets, governments can encourage voluntary sustainability disclosures and create incentives for private sector leadership in emissions monitoring and the adoption of the circular economy.

Blending formal and informal governance practices offers a realistic pathway to institutional development in emerging economies. Policymakers should formalise informal sector contributions through structured engagement and policy inclusion, while simultaneously strengthening regulatory agencies through resource allocation, capacity-building, and stakeholder trust-building. Institutional Theory suggests that governance models adapted to local institutional realities (rather than imposed from external paradigms) are more likely to secure enforcement capacity and legitimacy.

6.8 Conclusions and Policy Roadmap

In this chapter, we established that while regulatory frameworks form the foundation of circular economy and net-zero transitions in emerging markets, their functionality depends on a range of factors. Institutional weaknesses (e.g., fragmented regulations, limited enforcement capacity, and widespread informal sector dominance) persist as structural barriers. Institutional Theory elucidates how these deficits perpetuate governance voids and impede policy implementations. Evidence from Sub-Saharan Africa, Southeast Asia, and Latin America indicates that rigid, externally modelled regulations often fail in contexts where informal systems and community practices dominate environmental governance.

An effective transition to a circular economy and net-zero emissions requires multi-level, context-sensitive, and inclusive policy strategies. Policymakers must recognise that informal actors already sustain critical circular economy functions in many contexts, and that institutional legitimacy depends on engaging with these systems rather than displacing them. Governance models that blend formal regulatory oversight with structured integration of informal practices can enhance enforceability and policy credibility, particularly in countries where informal sectors control waste and resource flows.

A three-tiered policy roadmap emerges from this analysis:

At the national level, governments should prioritise fiscal incentives for sustainable production and consumption, introduce enforceable mandatory standards (such as eco-design regulations and recycling targets), and formally integrate informal sector actors into circular economy strategies through legal recognition, social protections, and technical support. Strengthening regulatory enforcement will require sustained investments in emissions monitoring infrastructure, data systems, and regulator capacity-building to enable credible oversight.

At the regional level, emerging economies can pursue a harmonised circular economy, net-zero certification standards, and coordinated capacity-building through knowledge-sharing platforms. Although frameworks such as the ASEAN Circular Economy Strategic Framework and the African Green Stimulus Programme are still in their early stages, they offer promising foundations for policy coherence and regional dialogue.

At the international level, emerging economies should prioritise coalition-building to strengthen collective negotiating positions in trade forums, such as the WTO. Strategic engagement must focus on mitigating risks by leveraging mechanisms such as the Carbon Border Adjustment Mechanism (CBAM) and securing enhanced access to climate finance and technical assistance. Simultaneously, integration of voluntary carbon markets and bilateral climate partnerships can provide critical resources for emissions reductions and reporting infrastructure.

References

African Union. (2022). *African Green Stimulus Programme*. https://agsp.nepad.org/

ASEAN Secretariat. (2021). *Framework for circular economy for the ASEAN Economic Community*. https://asean.org/wp-content/uploads/2021/10/Framework-for-Circular-Economy-for-the-AEC_Final.pdf

Baker, L. (2022). *The political economy of South Africa's carbon tax* (ICTD Working Paper 150). Institute of Development Studies. https://doi.org/10.19088/ICTD.2022.017

Barrie, J., Schröder, P., Schneider-Petsinger, M., King, R., & Benton, T. G. (2022). *The role of international trade in realizing an inclusive circular economy*. Chatham House. https://www.chathamhouse.org/sites/default/files/2022-10/2022-10-04-role-international-trade-inclusive-circular-economy-barrie-et-al.pdf

BloombergNEF. (2024). *Climatescope 2024: Emerging Markets Power Factbook*. https://www.global-climatescope.org/

Bloomberg. (2025). *Circular City Barometer*. https://sponsored.bloomberg.com/immersive/holcim/circular-cities/barometer

Byiers, B., & Medinilla, A. (2024). *The EU's Carbon Border Adjustment Mechanism and developing countries: Threats, opportunities and strategic responses*. European Centre for Development Policy Management. https://ecdpm.org/work/eus-carbon-border-adjustment-mechanism-and-developing-countries-threats-opportunities-and-strategic-responses

Chapungu, L., Nhamo, G., Chikodzi, D., & Maoela, M. A. (2022). BRICS and the race to net-zero emissions by 2050: Is COVID-19 a barrier or an opportunity? *Journal of Open Innovation: Technology, Market, and Complexity*, *8*(4), 172. https://doi.org/10.3390/joitmc8040172

CHINT. (2024). *CHINT Digital Carbon Management Platform has been certified*. https://www.chintglobal.com/global/en/about-us/news-center/news/chint-digital-carbon-management-platform-has-been-certified.html

da Silva, A. C., & Bermejo, R. (2023). MERCOSUR and environment: Progress in promoting the Sustainable Development Goals and the 2030 Agenda. *Revista Brasileira de Política Internacional*, *66*(2). https://doi.org/10.1590/0034-7329202300217

Dragomir, V. D., Dumitru, M., & Perevoznic, F. M. (2023). Carbon reduction and energy transition targets of the largest European companies: An empirical study based on institutional theory. *Cleaner Production Letters*, *4*, 100039. https://doi.org/10.1016/j.clpl.2023.100039

ESG Education. (n.d.). *Recognising waste pickers as part of the sustainability journey*. https://esg-edu.org/recognising-waste-pickers-as-part-of-the-sustainability-journey/

EU-ASEAN Business Council. (2024). *Charter of the ASEAN Circularity Coalition*. https://www.eu-asean.eu/wp-content/uploads/2024/03/EU-ABC-ASEAN-Circularity-Coalition-Charter-Final-19-03-24.pdf

European Commission. (2024). *CBAM frequently asked questions*. https://taxation-customs.ec.europa.eu/carbon-border-adjustment-mechanism_en

European Union. (2023). *Regulation (EU) 2023/956 establishing the Carbon Border Adjustment Mechanism*. https://eur-lex.europa.eu/legal-content/EN/TXT/?uri=CELEX%3A32023R0956

Gallego-Schmid, A., López-Eccher, C., Muñoz, E., Salvador, R., Cano-Londoño, N. A., Barros, M. V.,… & Guerrero, A. B. (2024). Circular economy in Latin America and the Caribbean: Drivers, opportunities, barriers and strategies. *Sustainable Production and Consumption*, *51*, 118–136.

Gallego-Schmid, A., Guerrero, A. B., Rebolledo-Leiva, R., Elorrieta-Mendoza, A., Paredes Cotohuanca, D. M., Tarpani, R. R. Z., Salvador, R., Barros, M. V., Henninger, C. E., & Vásquez-Ibarra, L. (2025). Social, Technological, Economic, and Policy Factors in the Circular Economy Transition in Brazil. *Sustainable Development*.

Hamerkop. (2025). *The most comprehensive carbon certification standards mapping on the market: 2024–25*. https://www.hamerkop.co/blog/infographics24-25

Hardi, I., Çoban, M. N., & Fumey, M. P. (2025). Innovation and carbon emissions: A Southeast Asian perspective. *Ekonomikalia Journal of Economics*, *3*(1). https://doi.org/10.60084/eje.v3i1.275

Henriksen, T. F. (2021, August 11). *Trash talk: Why the circular economy could be Sub-Saharan Africa's latest leapfrog industry*. NextBillion. https://nextbillion.net/trash-circular-economy-sub-saharan-africa-leapfrog-industry/

Indonesia Business Post. (2025, July 17). *Indonesia and BRICS hold the key to global energy transition: Report*. https://indonesiabusinesspost.com/4765/geopolitics-and-diplomacy/indonesia-and-brics-hold-the-key-to-global-energy-transition-report

Inter-American Development Bank. (2021). *Public-private partnerships in water and sanitation: Main figures and trends in Latin America and the Caribbean*. https://publications.iadb.org/publications/english/document/Public-Private-Partnerships-in-Water-and-Sanitation-Main-Figures-and-Trends-in-Latin-America-and-the-Caribbean.pdf

International Energy Agency. (2022). *An energy sector roadmap to net zero emissions in Indonesia*. https://iea.blob.core.windows.net/assets/b496b141-8c3b-47fc-adb2-90740eb0b3b8/AnEnergySectorRoadmaptoNetZeroEmissionsinIndonesia.pdf

International Monetary Fund. (2023). *South Africa: Selected issues* (Country Report No. 23/195). https://doi.org/10.5089/9798400245350.002

Maliszewska, M., Chepeliev, M., Fischer, C., & Jung, E. (2025, July 2). *How developing countries can measure exposure to the EU's carbon border adjustment mechanism*. The World Bank. https://blogs.worldbank.org/en/trade/how-developing-countries-can-measure-exposure-eus-carbon-border-adjustment-mechanism

MERCOSUR. (2021). *MERCOSUR countries together in climate change*. https://www.gov.br/mre/en/contact-us/press-area/press-releases/mercosur-countries-together-in-climate-change

Mugisha, E. K. (2025). Circular economy approaches for plastic waste management in Africa: Opportunities and challenges. *RIJEP*, *41*(P1), Article 4116. https://doi.org/10.59298/RIJEP/2025/4116

Murombedzi, J., & Munang, R. (2023). *Carbon markets for Africa: A primer*. UNECA & UNEP. https://akmh.uneca.org/sites/default/files/OIBC/4/Carbon%20Markets%20-%20A%20primer.pdf

Net Zero Policy Lab. (2025). *BRICS going green*. Johns Hopkins University.

Organisation for Economic Co-operation and Development (OECD). (2016). *OECD due diligence guidance for responsible supply chains of minerals from conflict-affected and high-risk areas* (3rd ed.). OECD Publishing. https://doi.org/10.1787/9789264252479-en

Organisation for Economic Co-operation and Development. (2025). *Climate action in Latin America: Data explainer*. https://www.oecd.org/en/data/insights/data-explainers/2025/02/climate-action-in-latin-america.html

Owojori, O. M., & Anwana, E. (2025). Climate governance in the BRICS: Pathways toward net-zero emissions. *Discover Sustainability*, *6*(359). https://doi.org/10.1007/s43621-025-01181-1

Pleeck, S., & Mitchell, I. (2023, November 15). *The EU's Carbon Border Tax: How can developing countries respond?* Center for Global Development. https://www.cgdev.org/blog/eus-carbon-border-tax-how-can-developing-countries-respond

Rasheed, K., Saad, S., Zaland, A., Khan, M. W., Ali, Z., Khan, M. H., Ammad, S., & Sadiq, T. (2024). Circular economy and critical barriers: Mapping the pathways and success metrics for sustainable circular success in industrialised South Asian developing nations. *Results in Engineering*, *24*, 102995. https://doi.org/10.1016/j.rineng.2024.102995

Reis-Filho, J. A., Gutberlet, J., & Giarrizzo, T. (2025). Invisible green guardians: A long-term study on informal waste pickers' contributions to recycling and the mitigation of greenhouse gas emissions. *Cleaner Waste Systems*, *10*, Article 100217. https://doi.org/10.1016/j.clwas.2025.100217

Ruth, C., & El-Amin, N. (2025). *Integrating circular economy principles in developing economies: Challenges and opportunities for Sub-Saharan Africa*. ResearchGate. https://www.researchgate.net/publication/390771658

Rweyendela, A. G., & Kombe, G. G. (2021). Institutional influences on circular economy: A Tanzanian perspective. *Sustainable Production and Consumption*, *26*, 1062–1073. https://doi.org/10.1016/j.spc.2021.01.013

Sembcorp. (2025). *Building Asia's low-carbon industrial future*. https://www.sembcorp.com/news-and-insights/insights-and-stories/corporate/building-asia-s-low-carbon-industrial-future

Sende, K. (2023). *International trade law and sustainability: Balancing trade liberalisation and environmental protection* [LLM Thesis]. University of Essex. https://www.researchgate.net/publication/377777171

Sovacool, B. K., Furszyfer Del Rio, D., & Zhang, W. (2023). The political economy of net-zero transitions: Policy drivers, barriers, and justice benefits to decarbonization in eight carbon-neutral countries. *Journal of Environmental Management, 347*, 119154. https://doi.org/10.1016/j.jenvman.2023.119154

United Nations Environment Programme (UNEP) & United Nations Economic Commission for Africa (UNECA). (n.d.). *Carbon markets for Africa: A primer*. https://akmh.uneca.org/sites/default/files/OIBC/4/Carbon%20Markets%20-%20A%20primer.pdf

United Nations Framework Convention on Climate Change (UNFCCC). (2025). *Updated NDC synthesis report*. https://unfccc.int/process-and-meetings/the-paris-agreement/nationally-determined-contributions-ndcs

Wang, Z. (2025). The impact of the Carbon Border Adjustment Mechanism (CBAM) on China's new energy vehicle exports to the European Union. *Journal of Economics, Management and Sustainability, 8*(2), 44–62. https://doi.org/10.30560/jems.v8n2p44

CHAPTER 7

Rethinking Governance for Circular Economy and Net-Zero Transitions in Emerging Markets: Conclusion and Recommendations

Abstract In this chapter, we consolidate the book's core findings, demonstrating that circular economy and net-zero transitions in emerging economies are fundamentally shaped by institutional conditions. While digital technologies and green finance mechanisms offer critical tools, their effectiveness depends on regulatory capacity, governance coherence, and institutional legitimacy. Drawing on institutional theory and regionally differentiated evidence from Sub-Saharan Africa, Southeast Asia, and Latin America, we highlight participatory governance, informal sector integration, and adaptive policymaking as foundational priorities. We present a multi-level, actionable policy roadmap, along with strategies for institutional strengthening, concluding that sustainable transitions require context-sensitive, inclusive, and capacity-focused governance reforms.

Keywords Circular economy · Net-Zero transition · Institutional theory · Emerging markets · Digital technologies · Participatory framework · Green finance · Policy roadmap

O. Evans and O. Adeola, *Innovations in Circular Economy and Net Zero*, https://doi.org/10.1007/978-3-032-22094-3_7

7.1 Introduction

In this concluding chapter, we synthesise the book's central insight: the adoption of circular economy practices and the transition to net-zero emissions in emerging markets are primarily institutional challenges, rather than technological or financial ones. While emerging technologies (e.g., AI, blockchain, digital twins) and financial instruments (e.g., green bonds, blended finance) offer essential tools, their effectiveness is contingent on the strength of institutional frameworks, regulatory coherence, and governance legitimacy that shape their implementation.

This analysis is grounded in institutional theory, which elucidates how regulatory fragmentation, limited enforcement capacity, and the persistent exclusion of informal systems hinder sustainability outcomes across Sub-Saharan Africa, Southeast Asia, and Latin America. However, this pattern is not uniform. Case studies from Vietnam and Brazil illustrate that coordinated national strategies, formalised cooperative structures, and credible reporting systems can facilitate progress, particularly when regulatory mandates are clear and institutional capacity is robust (IRRI, 2024; WWF, 2025). Consequently, institutional capacity and legitimacy emerge as key variables that explain policy divergence across regions.

This chapter draws together integrated lessons learned, framed through five analytical lenses: technological potential and limits, corporate leadership dependencies, financial mobilisation constraints, critical sectoral leverage points, and global policy pressures. The analysis underscores that global frameworks (e.g., the EU's Carbon Border Adjustment Mechanism (CBAM) and OECD due diligence standards) impose both regulatory constraints and offer strategic opportunities for emerging economies navigating global markets.

The remainder of this chapter, spanning Sects. 7.2–7.6, highlights key findings, proposes a comprehensive multi-level policy framework, reinterprets institutional theory in light of empirical evidence, and delineates future research priorities. A central theme is the imperative for adaptive, participatory, and context-sensitive institutional reforms. It is essential that participatory governance models, which incorporate informal systems, regional collaboration addressing shared constraints, and targeted capacity-building interventions, become foundational priorities for any credible circular and net-zero strategy in the Global South.

7.2 Lessons Learned: Integrated Reflections from the Book

7.2.1 *Digital Technologies: Potential and Limits*

Digital technologies such as AI, IoT, blockchain, and digital twins demonstrate considerable potential for enhancing resource efficiency and traceability across food, urban, and financial systems. In Vietnam, blockchain-supported traceability in rice straw reuse and mechanised agriculture underlines the feasibility of deploying digital tools within structured value chains (IRRI, 2024). Similarly, Southeast Asian EPR schemes leverage blockchain to meet recycling obligations under national regulations (TechInnovation, 2021). In the Limpopo River Basin, digital twin technology supports water resource management through real-time simulations and stakeholder scenario analysis (Garcia Andarcia et al., 2024).

However, digital adoption in emerging economies has been uneven. In Sub-Saharan Africa, weak digital infrastructure, skills deficits, and fragmented municipal data ecosystems hinder deployment (Oladosu et al., 2024). Latin American cities face interoperability challenges among municipal platforms, exacerbated by privacy regulations such as Brazil's General Data Protection Law (LGPD), which restrict data sharing necessary for effective AI modelling (IDB, 2024). In contrast, Vietnam's leadership stands out against the infrastructural constraints of African urban systems and the institutional fragmentation seen in Latin America.

Therefore, emerging markets should prioritise the development of regional digital innovation hubs to pool technical resources, share governance frameworks, and facilitate south–south technology adaptation (UNDP, 2024). Technologies must be modular, interoperable, and suited to low-infrastructure contexts. Without addressing these institutional and infrastructural foundations, digital circular economy tools risk deepening structural inequities rather than alleviating them.

7.2.2 *Corporate Leadership and Institutional Dependencies*

Corporate actors have a demonstrable capacity to drive circular innovation through closed-loop supply chains and sustainable product design. Southeast Asia's private sector participation in blockchain EPR platforms, as well as Vietnam's coordinated agricultural cooperatives, exemplify such potential (IRRI, 2024; TechInnovation, 2021). However, in many African and South Asian economies, firms face structural barriers, such as inconsistent policy environments, limited ESG disclosure mandates, and fragmented access to climate-aligned finance (Rasheed et al., 2024).

The analysis presented in this book demonstrates that effective corporate leadership is contingent upon stable regulatory frameworks and institutional incentives. Vietnam's coherent policy environment has facilitated corporate innovation, whereas the fragmented waste management system in Lagos has impeded private sector coordination (Oladosu et al., 2024). Consequently, it is imperative for governments to establish sector-specific public–private platforms, such as circular economy councils and industry consortia, to promote standardisation, knowledge exchange, and collective capacity-building (Sovacool et al., 2023). These platforms should also incorporate informal actors, given their critical role in resource recovery systems in numerous emerging economies (Sicam, 2023).

7.2.3 Green Finance: Untapped Yet Structurally Constrained

Green financial instruments (e.g., green bonds, blended finance, and sustainability-linked loans) are underdeveloped in most emerging markets. Nigeria's issuance of Africa's first sovereign green bond and Brazil's ESG-linked supervisory mandates illustrate early progress (WWF, 2025). However, their structural weaknesses persist. Inadequate green taxonomies, limited disclosure frameworks, and weak regulatory oversight undermine the credibility and scalability of green financial markets (FSD Africa, 2025). Project pipelines are also shallow, particularly at subnational levels (Nguyen et al., 2024).

The analysis confirms that complex instruments like blended finance are unsuitable for markets lacking foundational regulatory infrastructure. Policymakers should first establish national green funds to pool capital and de-risk early-stage projects (Demekas & Stallings, 2023). Disclosure frameworks, ESG integration, and sovereign-aligned project pipelines must become institutional priorities before attempting to scale private capital mobilisation (OECD, 2025; FSD Africa, 2025). Without credible reporting protocols and regulatory mandates, green finance risks remaining tokenistic rather than transformative.

7.2.4 *Sectoral Leverage Points for Circular Transitions*

Food systems and urban infrastructure are emerging as critical leverage points for advancing circularity. Vietnam's rice sector exemplifies how the integration of cooperatives, research institutes, and ministries can operationalise low-emission agriculture (IRRI, 2024). In contrast, cold chain innovations in Lagos address post-harvest losses but lack accompanying systemic governance reforms, thereby limiting their scalability (Okojie, 2023). Meanwhile, informal waste pickers in Manila illustrate the paradox of circular outcomes achieved outside formal governance frameworks (Sicam, 2023).

Institutional exclusion of informal actors constitutes a structural barrier. In both African urban waste systems and South Asian recycling industries, informal networks dominate material recovery but remain legally unrecognised (Rasheed et al., 2024). Consequently, participatory governance frameworks must become operational priorities. Governments should formalise informal actors by granting them legal status, providing technical training, and providing social protections to promote inclusivity in national circular strategies (Sicam, 2023; Sovacool et al., 2023). Failure to do so risks reinforcing socio-economic marginalisation and undermining the broader objectives of the circular economy.

7.2.5 *Policy, Trade, and International Engagement*

International trade governance is increasingly constraining the transition to a circular economy. The European Union's Carbon Border Adjustment Mechanism (CBAM) imposes financial obligations on carbon-intensive exports from countries such as Indonesia, thereby threatening industrial competitiveness in the absence of verified emissions reporting systems (Indonesia Business Post, 2025). Beyond CBAM, the OECD's due diligence frameworks and the WTO's stalled negotiations on environmental goods continue to exert procedural and compliance pressures on emerging economies (OECD, 2025; Sende, 2023). These frameworks effectively penalise markets that fail to meet transparency and reporting standards.

Therefore, integrating trade and climate policies must be a national strategic priority. Countries should invest in emissions monitoring infrastructure and align product certification systems with global regulatory expectations (Wang, 2025). Regional harmonisation of circular standards through ASEAN and the African Union can help mitigate market fragmentation, facilitate pooled issuance, and enhance regional competitiveness. Internationally, emerging markets should strengthen coalitions within WTO and UNFCCC negotiations to advocate for equitable frameworks, capacity-building, and market access (Murombedzi & Munang, 2023). Collective engagement remains the most viable strategy for negotiating global rules that currently reflect the priorities of developed economies.

7.3 Policy Roadmap: Multi-level Action Plan for Emerging Markets

The operationalisation of the circular economy and net-zero transitions in emerging markets demands context-sensitive, sequenced interventions across national, regional, and international levels. This roadmap synthesises insights from Sub-Saharan Africa, Southeast Asia, and Latin America, highlighting the need for institutional strengthening, participatory governance, and differentiated policy strategies.

7.3.1 National Level: Foundational Reforms and Institutional Strengthening

Prioritise Regulatory Foundations Before Market Instruments
National governments should first establish regulatory cornerstones, such as green taxonomies, ESG disclosure mandates, and sovereign-aligned project-reporting frameworks. Without these, attempts to scale green bonds or blended finance instruments risk exacerbating institutional fragmentation (FSD Africa, 2025; Demekas & Stallings, 2023). Governments must prioritise the integration of circular principles into fiscal policies, prudential regulations, and debt frameworks, as exemplified by Brazil and Nigeria (WWF, 2025).

Establish National Green Funds as First-Stage Financial Instruments
National green funds should function as de-risking instruments to mobilise public and private capital into climate-aligned investments. In countries with limited financial market sophistication, prematurely deploying blended finance mechanisms may be counterproductive.

Instead, the focus should be on publicly backed funds that can build robust project pipelines and enhance investor confidence (Demekas & Stallings, 2023).

Formalise Informal Sector Contributions Through Participatory Frameworks
Governments must legally recognise and support informal actors (e.g., waste pickers, smallholders, and local entrepreneurs) given their structural role in food and urban circular systems (Oladosu et al., 2024; Sicam, 2023). Legal recognition, social protection, and targeted training can transform informal systems from governance gaps into institutional assets.

Strengthen Emissions Monitoring and Digital Infrastructure as Strategic Prerequisites
National investments in emissions reporting infrastructure and interoperable data platforms are essential to meet both trade-compliance requirements and green-finance disclosure standards (Indonesia Business Post, 2025). Digital innovation hubs should prioritise modular, locally adapted technologies that ensure scalability, without overreliance on imported models (UNDP, 2024).

Enable Industry Participation Through Public–Private Platforms
Governments should establish sector-specific councils or knowledge-sharing consortia to standardise ESG practices, facilitate collective investment, and integrate both informal and formal enterprises (Sovacool et al., 2023). Private sector leadership depends not only on incentives but also on structured engagement and regulatory predictability.

7.3.2 Regional Level: Standards Harmonisation and Collective Capacity-Building

Adopt Differentiated Standards Harmonisation Strategies
Regional economic blocs should pursue the harmonisation of circular economy standards and verification systems, while recognising regional asymmetries. ASEAN can focus on refining implementation protocols, the African Union on developing basic standards, and CELAC on establishing foundational policy frameworks. Harmonisation efforts must prioritise adaptability to local institutional realities and avoid rigid model transfers.

Facilitate Regional Investment Aggregation Mechanisms
Pooling projects via joint green bond platforms or investment consortia can help smaller economies overcome scale limitations. Regional development banks and rating agencies should co-develop regional taxonomies, certification systems, as well as financial vehicles that align with international investors' expectations.

Strengthen South–South Knowledge Transfer Networks
Regional platforms must prioritise South–South cooperation in technological adaptation, regulatory models, and financing mechanisms. Technical exchanges (focused on modular digital technologies and informal sector integration) can help mitigate dependence on models from advanced economies (UNDP, 2024).

Formalise Private Sector and Informal Actor Engagement
Regional governance bodies should institutionalise stakeholder platforms that convene governments, private enterprises, informal sector representatives, and civil society. Integration of diverse actor perspectives will enhance policy legitimacy and support practical implementation pathways.

7.3.3 International Level: Strategic Engagement and Negotiation Capacity

Develop Integrated Trade–Climate Strategies
Emerging economies must align trade and climate policies to address the risks posed by instruments such as the CBAM and OECD supply chain frameworks (Indonesia Business Post, 2025). Building domestic emissions monitoring and certification capacity must precede trade negotiations to ensure credibility.

Prioritise Capacity-Building for Global Forum Participation
Meaningful engagement in WTO and UNFCCC negotiations requires institutional capacity, which many emerging markets currently lack (Sende, 2023). International partners and development agencies must support technical training and institutional strengthening to enable effective participation in rule-setting processes.

Expand Climate Finance and Carbon Market Access Through Structured Partnerships
National climate finance units should coordinate with multilateral donors to access the Green Climate Fund (GCF), Climate Investment Funds (CIF), and voluntary carbon markets (Murombedzi & Munang, 2023). Transparent reporting systems and standardised project proposals will aid in funding eligibility and allocation.

Negotiate Equitable Reporting Standards
Emerging economies should collectively advocate for reporting frameworks that recognise differentiated capabilities and avoid imposing rigid verification burdens. Emphasis on the inclusivity of global certification standards will protect local economic participation.

7.3.4 Cross-Cutting Principles: Institutional Theory-Informed Priorities

Sequence Reforms According to Institutional Readiness
Avoid overprescription of complex financial and regulatory tools in low-capacity contexts. Priority should be given to basic institutional strengthening before introducing advanced instruments or international compliance frameworks.

Promote Adaptive and Participatory Governance Models
Institutional legitimacy depends on the blending of formal oversight with structured engagement of informal actors. Rigid models transferred from advanced economies should be replaced by decentralised hybrid governance practices that reflect local institutional realities (Sovacool et al., 2023).

Centre Regulatory Capacity and Trust-Building
Policy effectiveness hinges on regulatory credibility. Governments must invest in both technical training and stakeholder trust-building, embedding sustainability mandates within fiscal and regulatory institutions as fiduciary priorities (Wongaree et al., 2025).

7.4 Institutional Theory: Rethinking Governance for Circularity and Net-Zero

Institutional theory explains why formal policy frameworks alone fail to deliver circular economy and net-zero transitions in many emerging markets. While advanced economies typically rely on coercive regulations, normative standards, and mimetic adoption to drive sustainability transformations (Dragomir et al., 2023), institutional fragmentation, informal sector dominance, and weak regulatory legitimacy shape governance outcomes across Sub-Saharan Africa, Southeast Asia, and Latin America (Ruth & El-Amin, 2025; Rweyendela & Kombe, 2021). This divergence underscores the need to fundamentally rethink governance models beyond regulatory transplantation. Across urban and agricultural systems, informal actors sustain critical circular functions yet remain institutionally marginalised. In urban centres across Africa and Asia, informal waste collectors dominate material recovery efforts (Sicam, 2023). In South Asia's circular industries, resource recovery relies on informal networks coordinated by local norms, rather than formal oversight (Rasheed et al., 2024). Institutional theory does not interpret these systems as governance voids, but rather as alternative institutional arrangements shaped by context-specific constraints and practices (Rweyendela & Kombe, 2021). Governance models that overlook these realities risk eroding policy legitimacy and weakening its enforcement.

Simultaneously, formal institutions (e.g., ministries, financial regulators, and development banks) play indispensable roles in structuring green finance, standardising reporting, and coordinating international engagement (FSD Africa, 2025). However, these agencies often lack the enforcement capacity and technical infrastructure to translate policies into credible action (Nguyen et al., 2024). Institutional theory emphasises that regulatory mandates, lacking perceived legitimacy or operational capacity, often yield symbolic compliance rather than substantive transformation (Rasheed et al., 2024).

Hybrid governance models offer a pragmatic alternative. As demonstrated by Bhutan and Gabon, decentralised and participatory structures that incorporate community practices can support climate objectives without relying solely on centralised enforcement (Sovacool et al., 2023). Blending formal oversight with structured informal engagement enables governments to progressively formalise existing circular practices through cooperative registration, technical assistance, and legal recognition. Vietnam's rice sector exemplifies how formal cooperatives, supported by national ministries, can integrate smallholders into formal circular systems without excluding traditional practices (IRRI, 2024).

Therefore, institutional strengthening must prioritise both capacity development and legitimacy building. Governments should invest in emissions monitoring infrastructure, regulatory coordination, and data systems, while simultaneously formalising informal sector contributions through participatory frameworks (Sicam, 2023). Institutional theory also explains that mimetic pressures (e.g., Nigeria's adoption of ICMA-aligned green bond standards) motivate policy adoption but do not guarantee implementation unless grounded in credible institutional environments (WWF, 2025).

Ultimately, circular and net-zero transitions are institutional processes, not merely technological or financial ones. Adaptive, participatory, and context-sensitive governance structures (rooted in local institutional logic and built upon regulatory capacity and stakeholder trust) offer the most viable pathway for emerging markets to embed sustainability within national development strategies.

7.5 Future Research Agenda

Future research must address specific knowledge gaps to support an effective circular economy and net-zero transition in emerging economies. First, longitudinal comparative studies are needed to understand how differing institutional contexts shape the long-term effectiveness of sustainability policies. While current research highlights cases of informal sector integration and regulatory reform (Rasheed et al., 2024; Sicam, 2023), future analyses should examine how informal–formal governance hybrids evolve, under what conditions they yield policy outcomes, and how institutional legitimacy interacts with enforcement capacity over time.

Second, the operational impact of digital technologies requires a targeted assessment. Emerging tools such as blockchain, AI, digital twins, and IoT systems offer significant scalability potential; however, their integration into governance structures is uneven (Garcia Andarcia et al., 2024). Future research should investigate how institutional capacity constraints (e.g., technical skills, data interoperability, and procedural governance) impact the adoption and effectiveness of these technologies.

Assessing whether digital innovations help reduce governance fragmentation or instead reinforce existing divides is particularly important for low-capacity urban and agricultural systems.

Third, trade governance requires deeper examination. While mechanisms such as CBAM and OECD reporting standards place significant pressure on exporters (Indonesia Business Post, 2025; OECD, 2025), little research has explored how trade-related institutional deficits restrict the participation of emerging markets in regulatory design and compliance. Investigating how trade capacity-building and regional cooperation can enhance negotiation leverage and market access would address the key policy blind spot.

Fourth, sector-specific research into corporate leadership is needed. The book identifies potential in the private sector for food systems, urban waste management, and sustainable finance; however, there is limited evidence on how firms navigate fragmented regulatory signals, ESG mandates, and restricted access to green finance. Comparative studies should examine how corporate strategies and public–private platforms interact with governance environments characterised by limited capacity and institutional fragmentation.

Finally, institutional theory should inform applied research on governance designs. Future studies should examine how legitimacy building, enforcement capacity, and hybrid governance models interact in practice, and identify adaptive institutional configurations that enable policy implementation in fragmented, resource-constrained settings. By addressing these applied research gaps, scholars and practitioners can design governance models that reflect the institutional realities of emerging economies pursuing circular and net-zero transitions.

7.6 Final Reflections

This book demonstrates that enabling a circular economy and net-zero transitions in emerging economies is a fundamental institutional challenge. While digital technologies, financial instruments, and international policy frameworks offer critical tools, their success depends on the quality and readiness of the domestic governance systems. Weak regulatory capacity, fragmented mandates, and limited coordination frequently undermine the scalability and credibility of sustainability policies across Sub-Saharan Africa, Southeast Asia, and Latin America. Yet, institutional capacities are uneven. Countries such as Vietnam and Brazil illustrate that coordinated regulatory frameworks, integrated financial oversight, and cooperative-based governance can enable circular transitions within credible institutional environments (IRRI, 2024; WWF, 2025).

The persistent exclusion of informal actors (e.g., waste pickers, smallholders, and informal entrepreneurs) is a structural limitation in many urban and agricultural systems. However, emerging evidence from Vietnam's rice cooperatives and community-based waste systems in Latin America shows that inclusive governance models can successfully formalise these actors (IRRI, 2024; Sicam, 2023). Institutional transformation must, therefore, centre participatory governance frameworks that blend formal mandates with structured informal engagement.

At the global level, emerging markets increasingly face regulatory pressure from mechanisms such as CBAM, OECD due diligence frameworks, and fragmented WTO environmental goods negotiations. These frameworks often reflect standards set by advanced economies, and impose compliance requirements that many emerging markets currently lack the institutional capacity to meet (Indonesia Business Post, 2025; OECD, 2025).

The final lesson is clear: technology adoption and financial innovation alone cannot deliver systemic transformation. Institutional strengthening must become a strategic foundation for circular and net-zero interventions. Governments should prioritise building regulatory capacity, credible reporting infrastructure, and inclusive participatory frameworks, before scaling complex financial or technological tools.

The circular economy and net-zero transitions must be understood as institutionally mediated processes. Adaptive, context-sensitive policymaking that values local governance realities, promotes regional cooperation, and incorporates legitimacy into institutional mandates offers the most realistic pathway for emerging markets to achieve equitable, scalable, and climate-resilient futures.

References

Demekas, D., & Stallings, J. A. (2023). *Challenges of green finance—Private sector perspectives from emerging markets*. World Bank. http://documents.worldbank.org/curated/en/099717411212328052

Dragomir, V. D., Dumitru, M., & Perevoznic, F. M. (2023). Carbon reduction and energy transition targets of the largest European companies: An empirical study based on institutional theory. *Cleaner Production Letters, 4*, 100039.

FSD Africa. (2025). *Impact of green bonds in Africa*. https://fsdafrica.org/wp-content/uploads/2025/05/Green-Bond-Report_Final-report-20.03.2025.pdf

Garcia Andarcia, M., Dickens, C., Silva, P., Matheswaran, K., & Koo, J. (2024). *Digital Twin for management of water resources in the Limpopo River Basin: A concept*. International Water Management Institute (IWMI). https://cgspace.cgiar.org/server/api/core/bitstreams/f3fd37c9-bb7f-4503-bffd-5a4a1bf26383/content

IDB. (2024, September). *Digital transformation of solid waste management: Waste collection innovation, business intelligence, and digital technologies to transition waste management towards circularity in Latin America and the Caribbean* (Technical Note No. IDB-TN-0301). Inter-American Development Bank. https://publications.iadb.org/en/publications/english/viewer/technical-note-no-idb-tn-0301-vf.pdf

Indonesia Business Post. (2025, July 17). *Indonesia and BRICS hold the key to global energy transition: Report*. https://indonesiabusinesspost.com/4765/geopolitics-and-diplomacy/indonesia-and-brics-hold-the-key-to-global-energy-transition-report

IRRI. (2024, July 23). *Vietnam's pilot low-emission rice farming shows promise: Increased yields, profits and sustainability*. International Rice Research Institute. https://www.cgiar.org/news-events/news/vietnams-pilot-low-emission-rice-farming-shows-promise increased-yields-profits-and-sustainability/

Murombedzi, J., & Munang, R. (2023). *Carbon markets for Africa: A primer*. UNECA & UNEP. https://akmh.uneca.org/sites/default/files/OIBC/4/Carbon%20Markets%20-%20A%20primer.pdf

Nguyen, P.-H., Nguyen, L.-A.T., Le, H.-Q., & Tran, L.-C. (2024). Navigating critical barriers for green bond markets using a fuzzy multi-criteria decision-making model: Case study in Vietnam. *Heliyon, 10*(13), e33493. https://doi.org/10.1016/j.heliyon.2024.e33493

OECD. (2025). Sustainable bonds. In *Asia Capital Markets Report 2025*. https://www.oecd.org/en/publications/asia-capital-markets-report-2025_02172cdc-en/full-report/sustainable-bonds_21e9a353.html

Okojie, J. (2023, March 29). *Ecotutu to launch cold chain infrastructure to tackle post-harvest losses*. BusinessDay. https://businessday.ng/agriculture/article/ecotutu-to-launch-cold-chain-infrastructure-to-tackle-post-harvest-losses/

Oladosu, O., Abiodun, O. A., Oloruntoba, E. O., & Adegoroye, A. (2024). *Evaluating urban service delivery in Lagos State Nigeria: A bid to enhance sustainable waste management*. ResearchGate. https://www.researchgate.net/publication/378526141

Rasheed, K., Saad, S., Zaland, A., Khan, M. W., Ali, Z., Khan, M. H., Ammad, S., & Sadiq, T. (2024). Circular economy and critical barriers: Mapping the pathways and success metrics for sustainable circular success in industrialised

South Asian developing nations. *Results in Engineering, 24*, 102995. https://doi.org/10.1016/j.rineng.2024.102995
Ruth, C., & El-Amin, N. (2025). *Integrating circular economy principles in developing economies: Challenges and opportunities for Sub-Saharan Africa*. ResearchGate. https://www.researchgate.net/publication/390771658
Rweyendela, A. G., & Kombe, G. G. (2021). Institutional influences on circular economy: A Tanzanian perspective. *Sustainable Production and Consumption, 26*, 1062–1073. https://doi.org/10.1016/j.spc.2021.01.013
Sende, K. (2023). *International trade law and sustainability: Balancing trade liberalisation and environmental protection* [LLM Thesis]. University of Essex. https://www.researchgate.net/publication/377777171
Sicam, O. (2023). The production of space in the informal waste economy: Waste picking in the Tondo Manila Bay Area. *The Journal of Public Space, 8*(1), 43–68. https://doi.org/10.32891/jps.v8i1.1212
Sovacool, B. K., Furszyfer Del Rio, D., & Zhang, W. (2023). The political economy of net-zero transitions: Policy drivers, barriers, and justice benefits to decarbonization in eight carbon-neutral countries. *Journal of Environmental Management, 347*, 119154. https://doi.org/10.1016/j.jenvman.2023.119154
TechInnovation. (2021). *A platform to commercially scale plastic recycling*. https://na.eventscloud.com/website/30321/a-platform-to-commercially-scale-plastic-recycling/
UNDP. (2024). *Carbon markets in Africa: Balancing finance mobilisation with emission reduction goals*. https://www.undp.org/africa/blog/carbon-markets-africa-balancing-finance-mobilization-emission-reduction-goals
Wang, Z. (2025). The impact of the Carbon Border Adjustment Mechanism (CBAM) on China's new energy vehicle exports to the European Union. *Journal of Economics, Management and Sustainability, 8*(2), 44–62. https://doi.org/10.30560/jems.v8n2p44
Wongaree, P., Chiyachantana, C. N., Ding, D. K., Prasarnphanich, P., & Siwasarit, W. (2025). The pricing of green bonds and the determinants of the green bond premium in the Asia-Pacific and European markets. *Journal of Open Innovation: Technology, Market, and Complexity, 11*(2), 100546. https://doi.org/10.1016/j.joitmc.2025.100546
WWF. (2025). *Banks in Africa and Latin America can lead green growth and transition*. https://wwf.panda.org/?13985416/Banks-in-Africa-and-Latin-America-can-lead-green-growth-and-transition

Index

O. Evans and O. Adeola, *Innovations in Circular Economy and Net Zero*, https://doi.org/10.1007/978-3-032-22094-3

The manufacturer's authorised representative in the EU is Springer Nature Customer Service Centre GmbH, Europaplatz 3, 69115 Heidelberg, Germany. If you have any concerns regarding our products, please contact ProductSafety@springernature.com

Printed and bound by CPI Group (UK) Ltd, Croydon, CR0 4YY

17/09/2026

02218454-0001